THE BASIS AND
ESSENTIALS OF
GERMAN

THE BASIS AND ESSENTIALS OF
GERMAN

Containing all that must be known of
Grammar, Vocabulary and Idioms for
most everyday purposes by
CHARLES DUFF and **RICHARD FREUND**
Fourth edition, revised and partly rewritten

NELSON

THOMAS NELSON AND SONS LTD
36 Park Street London W1
P.O. Box 336 Apapa Lagos
P.O. Box 25012 Nairobi
P.O. Box 21149 Dar es Salaam
P.O. Box 2187 Accra
77 Coffee Street San Fernando Trinidad

THOMAS NELSON (AUSTRALIA) LTD
597 Little Collins Street Melbourne 3000

THOMAS NELSON AND SONS (SOUTH AFRICA) (PROPRIETARY) LTD
51 Commissioner Street Johannesburg

THOMAS NELSON AND SONS (CANADA) LTD
81 Curlew Drive Don Mills Ontario

THOMAS NELSON AND SONS
Copewood and Davis Streets Camden New Jersey 08103

First published 1933
Fourth edition extensively revised
with new Essential Vocabulary 1969

17 146063 4

Made and printed in Great Britain by
William Clowes and Sons, Limited, London and Beccles
for Thomas Nelson and Sons Ltd, 36 Park Street, London W1

PREFACE TO THIS EDITION

The *Basis and Essentials of German* was first published in 1933, revised in 1935, and again in 1945.* Those editions were many times reprinted. The main object of the book was and still is this: to provide a minimal statement of German grammar, which, when supplemented by carefully chosen essential vocabulary, would enable whoever assimilated this limited material to deal with those requirements of everyday life which recur most frequently.

Advances in the new science of linguistics, especially since the end of the Second World War, are a factor in the need for a new and more fully revised edition of this book. Besides, many more English-speaking people now visit the German-speaking countries, and obviously their special needs would have to be taken into consideration, which means the addition of a number of special words to the 'Essential Vocabulary'.

It was with these objectives in mind that the revision was undertaken. The whole vocabulary has been revised, improved, and enlarged. As for the grammar in Part I of the book, this has been left almost as it was, apart from corrections and a few amendments. In favour of retaining the original streamlined statement of grammar on orthodox lines is the simple fact that no better method of presenting the most frequently recurring complexities of German grammar has yet been devised. It is still the most economical, possibly the most logical, and certainly the easiest to master. Instead of adding immediately unnecessary lists of exceptions to rules, the most important exceptions are noted under the relevant word in the Vocabulary at the end of the book. They can be learnt piecemeal as they are met, or at some later stage—after the fundamental principles have been assimilated.

It is strange that German scholarship has not yet achieved a modern basic vocabulary on scientific lines for German. There is nothing authoritative in German to parallel the 1,350 words of *Le Français Fondamental* that was produced under the auspices of the French Ministry of National Education over ten years ago. The most encouraging efforts on behalf of German are the American

* And now again in 1969.—*Ed.*

Word Frequency Dictionary compiled by H. S. Eaton,* and the *Basic (Spoken) German Word List* by J. Alan Pfeffer. We acknowledge with gratitude the help we have found in these works, which have caught within their net some useful words missing from the earlier editions of ours but now thankfully included here. Our original 'Essential Vocabulary' consisted of just over 1,200 words, nearly all of which are again included. The remaining words are those which are most likely to be required by the traveller, the motorist and the visitor to German-speaking countries, as well as by the general student who wishes to acquire many words of everyday practical utility. Our total vocabulary now approaches 3,000 words, phrases, and idioms: this, with the grammar in pages 8–62, contains what may be regarded as the fundamental material required by every person wishing to have more than a mere smattering of the language. It will carry him or her a long way. It is also material of primary importance which every serious student must master before hoping to advance very far in his studies.

Although not particularly designed for use in class teaching, earlier editions were successfully used for this purpose, which requires enthusiasm and extra work on the part of the teacher, who has to devise his own exercises and methods of practice. The present edition should be much better for use in either class or individual tuition. Criticisms and suggestions will be welcomed and should be addressed to the General Editorial Department, Thomas Nelson & Sons Ltd., 36 Park Street, London W.1.

CHARLES DUFF,
RICHARD FREUND.

* An English–French–German–Spanish *Word Frequency Dictionary* compiled by Helen S. Eaton. Copyright 1940. Published by Dover Publications, Inc., New York, 1961, and by Constable & Co. Ltd., London. The original edition was issued by the Committee on Modern Languages of the American Council of Education.

CONTENTS

PART II
THE ESSENTIAL VOCABULARY

PART III
EXTRACTS TO ILLUSTRATE THE USE AND
SCOPE OF THE VOCABULARY AND
GRAMMAR

PART I

THE BASIS OF GRAMMAR

THE FUNDAMENTAL MATERIAL OF GERMAN

For most practical purposes, the fundamental material of German consists of a comparatively small number of selected words with enough grammar to make them work.

In Part I of this book the grammar has been simplified down to basic requirements. All of Part I must be known—and known thoroughly. In it a number of words show how the grammar works, and these examples must be memorized before approaching Part II.

Part II consists of the Essential Vocabulary—a total of about 2,700 words, idioms, and phrases.

In Part III (pages 111–117) are Extracts for Reading which illustrate the scope and wide-ranging utility of the fundamental material given in Parts I and II. The translations given with them fill in the meanings of the few words which have not been included in the Essential Vocabulary.

The fundamental material presented in this book includes nothing that is not likely to be required for a minimum working knowledge of the language or as a foundation for further study.

ALPHABET AND PRONUNCIATION

The alphabet is the same as in English, but German is printed in both Gothic and Latin characters; and there is a special script for writing. The beginner is advised not to worry himself greatly with either Gothic type or script during the first weeks of learning. It is surprising how soon one becomes quite at home with the Gothic: facility in reading comes almost without effort, once a little headway has been made with the language. As for the handwriting, this should definitely be avoided until this book is well known. Handwriting in Latin characters is taught in all German schools, and in printed matter Latin characters have become increasingly popular for general use.

For purposes of reference, however, here is the Gothic alphabet with the Latin equivalents and the names of the letters underneath:

𝔄 𝔞	𝔅 𝔟	ℭ 𝔠	𝔇 𝔡	𝔈 𝔢	𝔉 𝔣	𝔊 𝔤
A a	*B b*	*C c*	*D d*	*E e*	*F f*	*G g*
ah	*beh*	*tsay*	*day*	*eh*	*eff*	*gay*

ℌ 𝔥	ℑ {i/j}	𝔎 𝔨	𝔏 𝔩	𝔐 𝔪	𝔑 𝔫	𝔒 𝔬
H h	*I i, J j*	*K k*	*L l*	*M m*	*N n*	*O o*
hah	*ee, yot*	*kah*	*ell*	*em*	*en*	*oh*

𝔓 𝔭	𝔔 𝔮	𝔯 𝔯	𝔖 ſ s[1]	𝔗 𝔱	𝔘 𝔲	𝔙 𝔳
P p	*Q q*	*R r*	*S s*	*T t*	*U u*	*V v*
pay	*koo*	*air*	*ess*	*tay*	*oo*	*fow*

𝔚 𝔴	𝔛 𝔵	𝔜 𝔶	ℨ 𝔷			
W w	*X x*	*Y y*	*Z z*			
vay	*ix*	*üpsilon*	*tsett*			

𝔠𝔥 𝔠𝔥	𝔠𝔨	𝔖𝔠𝔥 𝔰𝔠𝔥	ſʒ	ſſ	𝔱𝔷
ch	*ck*	*sch*	*sz*[2]	*ss*	*tz*

Modified vowels	𝔄 ä	𝔒 ö	𝔘 ü

There are no 'accents' as in French, for example, but only the diaeresis (¨) which is used to 'modify' all sounds of the vowels

---

[1] ſ is used only at the end of a word or syllable.
[2] ß or ss is always used instead of sz in Latin type.

a, **o, u** and the diphthong **au** when written **Ä, ä, Ö, ö, Ü, ü, Äu, äu,** to be pronounced in the manner described later.

VOWEL SOUNDS

A vowel is long when it is doubled (**aa, ee, oo**): **das Boot** *boat*; when it comes before a single consonant followed by a vowel (**eben** *even*); or when it is followed by the letter **h** (**der Sohn** *son*); also often before a single final consonant (**gut** *good*); **ß** and **ch** count as one consonant.

A vowel is short when it comes before two or more consonants (**besser** *better*, **erst** *first*). The letter **e** at the end of a word and in the endings **-el, -en, -er** is always short (**Katze** *cat*, **Singer** *singer*).

German sounds must be clearly made. They are:

Long A—like English *a* in *father*:	der **Vater** *father*
Short A—like Northern English *a* in *man*:	der **Mann** *man*
Long E—like French *é* in *Élise*: (closed)	der **Esel** *donkey*
Long Ä—as in English *fair*: (open)	der **Bär** *bear*
Short E—like English *e* in *net, bet*:	**wenn** *when*, die **Hände** *hands*
Unstressed E—as in English *begin*:	der **Beginn** *beginning*, der **Handel** *trade*
Long I—as in English *machine*:	das **Fieber** *fever* die **Musik** *music*
Short I—like English *i* in *miss, sit*:	das **Kind** *child*
Long O—similar to *o* in Scots *road*:	der **Ofen** *stove* das **Boot** *boat*
Short O—like English *o* in *not, pot*:	die **Woche** *week*
Long U—as in English *loom*:	das **Blut** *blood*
Short U—like English *oo* in *foot*:	die **Butter** *butter*
Long Ö—like French *eu* in *jeune*:	der **Löwe** *lion*, das **Öl** *oil*
Short Ö—similar to *œ* in French *sœur*:	die **Hölle** *hell*
Long Ü—as in French *rue*:	die **Übung** *exercise*
Short Ü—similar to long Ü, but pronounced more sharply:	der **Müller** *miller*

Note: The letter **y** which appears as a vowel in loan-words is usually pronounced **ü**: der **Typ** *type*.

DIPHTHONGS

AI, AY, EI, EY are almost like English *ei* in *height*

der Kaiser *emperor*　　**Bayern** *Bavaria*
nein *no*　　　　　　　 **Meyer** (*surname*)
　　　　　reich *rich*

AU is rather like English *ou* in *house*, but broader (ah-oo):
　　　das Haus *house*

ÄU and **EU** are like *oy* in *boy*:
　　neu *new*　　　　　 **die Häuser** *houses*

CONSONANTS

Unless mentioned below, consonants are pronounced more or less as in English.

B　　　　at the end of a word or word-syllable is unvoiced and resembles *p*: **der Dieb** *thief*, **die Abteilung** *department*.

CH　　　after **a, o, u, au** resembles the *ch* in Scots *loch*: **das Buch** *book*, **auch** *also*.
　　　　　Otherwise it is softer and a palatal sound: **ich** *I*, **das Mädchen** *girl*, **die Chemie** *chemistry*.

D　　　　at the end of a word or word-syllable is unvoiced, like *t*: **das Pfund** *pound*, **der Handschuh** *glove*.

G　　　　is hard as in *go, get*: **gehen** *to go*.
　　　　　At the end of a word or word-syllable **g** is unvoiced, like *k*: **der Tag** *day*, **das Flugzeug** *aeroplane*.
　　　　　The suffix **-ig** is pronounced like **-ich**: **der König** *king*, **die Ewigkeit** *eternity*.

-NG　　is like Southern English *ng* in *sing*: **der Ring** *ring*

-NGER　is always like *-nger* in Southern English *singer* (never as in English *finger*).

H　　　　is mute after any vowel, otherwise it is strongly voiced: **sehr** *very*, **hundert** *hundred*.

J　　　　is like English *y*: **der Jäger** *huntsman*, **jung** *young*.

K　　　　is never silent in words like: **der Knabe** *boy*, **das Knie** *knee*.

L　　　　is 'liquid' as in French and not 'dark' as in English.

PF　　　both letters are sounded: **die Pflanze** *plant*.

QU　　　is like English *kv*: **die Quelle** *source*.

R　　　　is quite unlike English *r*. It is always 'gargled' or trilled.

S	before and between vowels is like English *z*: **die Rose** *rose*, **der Sohn** *son*.
SCH	is like English *sh*: **die Schule** *school*.
SP & ST	at the beginning of a word or word-syllable are like English *shp*, *sht*: **sprechen** *to speak*, **stehen** *to stand*.
-TION	is like English *tseeóhn*: **die Nation** *nation*.
V	is like English *f*: **der Vater** *father*.
W	is like English *v*: **der Wein** *wine*, **das Wasser** *water*.
Z	is like *ts* in English *rats*: **schwarz** *black*. Tz is similarly pronounced: **die Katze** *cat*.

ORTHOGRAPHY

All nouns are written with a capital letter, whatever their position in a sentence: **Singt der Mann?** *Does the man sing?*

All adjectives, even those of nationality, are written with small letters. **Es ist deutsch.** *It is German.*

Except at the beginning of a sentence **ich** *I* is written with a small letter.

Sie and **Ihr**, meaning *you* and *your*, are written with capitals, to distinguish them from **sie, ihr** *they*, *their* (or *she, her*). In personal correspondence **Du, Dich, Dein** and **Ihr, Euch, Euer** are written with capitals.

Every German word is written as it is pronounced and pronounced as it is written. Double 's'; ss, is written ß except between two vowels of which the first is short:

> **der Gruß** *greeting*,   **die Grüße** *greetings*
> **besser** *better*,   **die Flüsse** *rivers*

STRESS

One syllable of every German word is stressed more heavily than the others. This is the 'root' syllable and, as a general rule, it is the *first*. In compound words the stress is usually on the first component. Stress can best be learnt from a teacher or by hearing.

German pronunciation is more definite, more vigorous, more distinct than English. Syllables are clear-cut. There is no mumbling, slurring, or drawling such as we have in Southern English. To English people Germans make what appears to be an exaggerated use of tongue, lips, and vocal apparatus generally.

Warning

It should be clearly understood that the equivalents for pronunciation given above are makeshifts. Strictly, every letter or combination of letters should be considered to represent a sound or sounds which have no exact equivalents in English. Good pronunciation can only be learnt from good native speakers. Gramophone records are helpful, but German radio broadcasts, especially those from North-German stations, and tape-recordings, provide marvellous opportunities for learning the sounds of the language. Listen carefully and imitate the speaker. This will soon give facility. There is hardly an excuse nowadays for not *hearing* as much of it as is required.

The foreign learner must aim to speak good, clear German so that he will be understood, and to understand the language when he hears it spoken. Practice in speaking with good native speakers is an essential if the goal is to be achieved.

DECLENSION

German is what grammarians call a synthetic language. By this they mean that it prefers to make compound and derivative words[1] and to use endings and inflexions instead of making a liberal use of particles as the 'analytic' languages do—English, for example. As will be seen later, articles, nouns, adjectives, and pronouns change their endings to convey different meanings, and this process is called *declension*. It hardly exists in English.

Articles, nouns, adjectives, and pronouns have four 'cases' in both the singular and the plural. All except nouns have changes for the three genders (masculine, feminine, and neuter).

The four cases are: nominative, genitive, dative, and accusative.

1. *The nominative* names the *subject*, or initiator of action, speech, etc.
2. *The genitive* indicates the *possessor* of something.
3. *The dative* indicates the *recipient* of something—the indirect object of action or speech.
4. *The accusative* is used for *direct object*, the person or thing which directly receives the action.

Thus: *I gave John's hat to Tom.*

I is **nominative.**	Answers the question:			Who?
John's is **genitive**	,,	,,	,,	Whose?
Tom is **dative**	,,	,,	,,	To whom?
hat is **accusative**	,,	,,	,,	Whom, What?

It is impossible to make any progress in German until the simple use of the cases is understood. Declension in German is important and, for nouns, fairly complicated. That of articles, adjectives, and pronouns is regular and fixed. It is pardonable to make mistakes in the declensions of nouns but the remainder—articles, adjectives, pronouns—need not cause great trouble. It is a question of *repetition* until they are mastered.

Ingenious writers of text-books have invented many tricks and so-called short-cuts to expound the German declensions. It is, however, our firm conviction that the old, orthodox, and straight-

---

[1] See pp. 58–62 on Word-building.

forward method is the simplest of them all. In the pages which follow, the very minimum necessary to express the most frequently recurring ideas will be given. It should be regarded as a basis upon which to build.

ARTICLES

The words *the* and *a* are called articles, the former the definite, the latter the indefinite article. The former is declined in German, in both singular and plural; the latter, by its nature, only the singular.

DEFINITE ARTICLES DECLINED

The table on page 11 shows the declension of the definite articles and of **dies-** *this*, **welch-** *which*.

Jen- *that*, **jed-** *each* and **manch-** *many a* also decline in this way.

INDEFINITE ARTICLE DECLINED

The table on page 12 shows the declension of the indefinite article and of **kein** *no, not a*, and **mein-** *my*.

The remaining possessive adjectives also follow this pattern.

| | SINGULAR | | | PLURAL |
	MASCULINE	FEMININE	NEUTER	MASC FEM NEUT
NOMINATIVE	ER Der Direktor ist hier. Dieser Mann ist alt. Welcher Wagen gehört Ihnen?	E Die Milch kocht. Diese Kirche ist alt. Welche Schule ist neu?	(E)S Das Flugzeug fliegt ab. Dieses Kind weint. Welches Kino ist neu?	E Die Männer warten. Diese Damen warten auch. Welche Kinder weinen?
GENITIVE	ES Ich bin ein Freund des Direktors. Sind Sie ein Freund dieses Mannes?	ER Das ist der Mann der Sekretärin. Wo ist die Tasche dieser Dame?	ES Die Fenster des Büros sind kaputt. Die Eltern dieses Kindes sind tot.	ER Die Arbeit der Damen ist gut. Die Mütter dieser Kinder kommen morgen.
DATIVE	EM Ich gebe es dem Lehrer. Ich gebe diesem Mann(e) Geld. Welchem Mann(e) gibst du es?	ER Wie geht's der Lehrerin? Es geht dieser Dame schlecht. Welcher Dame gibst du es?	EM Wie geht's dem Kind(e)? Ich gebe es diesem Fräulein. Welchem Fräulein geht es schlecht?	EN Gibst du es den Kindern? Was geben Sie diesen Männern? Welchen Damen geht es gut?
ACCUSATIVE	EN Ich besuche den Direktor. Ich kenne diesen Mann. Welchen Freund bringst du?	E Ich kenne die Tochter. Ich kaufe diese Lampe. Welche Tasche kaufst du?	(E)S Ich kaufe das Haus. Ich kenne dieses Fräulein. Welches Buch nehmen Sie?	E Ich kaufe die Stühle. Ich kaufe diese Lampen. Welche Schuhe kaufst du?

| | SINGULAR | | | PLURAL |
	MASCULINE	FEMININE	NEUTER	MASC FEM NEUT
NOMINATIVE	— Ein Bruder ist ein Mann. Kein Bruder ist eine Frau. Mein Bruder ist jung.	E Eine Schwester ist eine Frau. Keine Schwester ist ein Mann. Meine Schwester ist jung.	— Ein Haus ist ein Gebäude. Kein Haus ist billig. Mein Haus ist neu.	E Keine Brüder sind hier. Meine Schwestern sind nett.
GENITIVE	ES Das Leben eines Studenten ist leicht. Das Leben keines Studenten ist schwer. Das Auto meines Bruders ist draußen.	ER Das Leben einer Frau ist schwer. Das Leben keiner Frau ist leicht. Der Roller meiner Schwester ist draußen.	ES Das Weinen eines Kindes. Das Leben keines Kindes. Die Schule meines Kindes ist neu.	ER Die Freunde meiner Schwestern sind alle nett.
DATIVE	EM Er gibt einem Mann(e) Geld. Sie gibt keinem Mann(e) Geld. Ich gebe meinem Bruder Wein.	ER Ich gebe alles einer Frau. Ich gebe keiner Frau Geld. Er gibt meiner Schwester einen Ring.	EM Sie gibt einem Kind 10 Pf. Ich gebe keinem Kind(e) Geld Er gibt meinem Kind(e) DM 1.	E Wir geben keinen Männern Geld. Er gibt meinen Schwestern Geld.
ACCUSATIVE	E Ich habe einen Bruder. Sie hat keinen Bruder. Sie liebt meinen Bruder.	E Ich habe eine Schwester. Sie hat keine Schwester. Er liebt meine Schwester.	— Ich habe ein Haus. Sie hat kein Haus. Ich verkaufe mein Haus.	E Sie hat keine Brüder. Er kennt meine Schwestern.

DIFFERENT USAGE OF ARTICLES IN GERMAN AND ENGLISH

The definite article is often required in German when English does not require it:

days of the week	**am** Montag *on Monday(s)*
months of the year	**im** Dezember *in December*
names of seasons	**im** Frühling *in Spring*
abstract nouns	**Die** Zeit vergeht schnell. *Time passes quickly.*
names of streets, squares, and lakes	in **der** Kaiserstraße *on Kaiser Street*
	am Paulsplatz *at St. Paul's Square*
	am Bodensee *on Lake Constance*
sometimes with parts of the body or clothing	Er nimmt **den** Hut ab. *He takes off his hat.*
	Ich wasche mir **das** Gesicht. *I'm washing my face.*
proper noun preceded by an adjective	**das** schöne Deutschland *beautiful Germany*
	der junge Albert *young Albert*
place-names which are not neuter	in **der** Schweiz *in Switzerland*
	Freiburg **im** Bresgau

Also in such expressions as:

> in **der** Stadt *in town*
> **zur** Schule *to school*
> **ins** Kino gehen *to go to the cinema*
> mit **dem** Bus *by bus*
> **im** allgemeinen *in general*

The article is *not* required in German:

before nouns (not qualified by an adjective) denoting profession or nationality	Er ist Deutscher. *He is a German.* Ich bin Arzt. *I'm a doctor.*
after **alle** and **beide**	**alle** Jungen *all (the) boys* **beide** Brüder *both (the) brothers*

in such expressions as:

> **Ende** April *at the end of April*
> **Anfang** Mai *at the beginning of May*
> **Mitte** März *in the middle of March*

Contractions of the Article

an das → ans	in dem → im
an dem → am	von dem → vom
bei dem → beim	zu dem → zum
in das → ins	zu der → zur

NOUNS

GENDER

There are three genders in German: masculine, feminine, and neuter, but they do not follow the simple English rules of gender, as will be seen.

General rule: Nouns denoting males are masculine, and those denoting females are feminine.

But note: **das Mädchen** *girl*, **die Waise** *orphan* (male or female), **die Schildwache** *sentinel.*

The feminine of many male nouns is formed by adding **-in** to the masculine: **der König** *king*, **die Königin** *queen.*

Hints worth noting and for reference

Masculine are:

Names of seasons, months, days of the week, winds, points of the compass.

Der Stein *stone*, and all other stones.

Nouns ending in **-ling**, **-ich**, **-ig**; nouns derived from verbs and ending **-er** and **-el** (**der Flügel** *wing*, from **fliegen** *to fly*).

Nouns of one syllable formed from roots of verbs (**der Biß** *bite*, from **beißen** *to bite*).

Note: **der Mond** *moon.*

Feminine are:

Names of most trees, flowers, small animals, insects, etc. (**die Maus** *mouse*, **die Ratte** *rat*, **die Mücke** *midge*).

Nouns ending in **-ei**, **-in**, **-heit**, **-keit**, and **-schaft**, **-ung**, **-ie**, **-ik**, **-ion**, **-tät** (the last four often of foreign origin).

Nouns ending **-e** derived from adjectives or verbs (**die Länge** *length*, from **lang** *long*; **die Höhe** *height*, from **hoch** *high*).

Most nouns ending **-t** derived from verbs (**die Macht** *might*, from **mögen** *to be able*; **die Schrift** *writing*, from **schreiben** *to write*; **die Tat** *deed*, from **tun** *to do*).

Exception: **der Rat** *advice*, from **raten** *to advise*.
Note: **die Sonne** *the sun*.

Neuter are:

Names of countries and places (**Deutschland, Berlin**), with few
exceptions, e.g. **die Schweiz** *Switzerland*.
Names of metals (**das Gold**).
All verbs used as nouns (**das Singen** *singing*).
Most nouns ending in **-tum, -sal, -sel** (but note **die Mühsal** *trouble*).
Most collective nouns beginning with **ge-** (**das Gebirge** *range of
mountains*, **das Gespräch** *conversation*).
All diminutives in **-chen** and **-lein** (**das Mädchen** *girl*).

Compound nouns:

These take the gender of the last component (**die Tasche** *pocket*,
das Tuch *cloth, rag*: **das Taschentuch** *handkerchief*).

Remember, however, that those compounds of **der Mut** *spirit*
which denote the kindlier and gentler qualities are *feminine*: **die
Sanftmut** *gentleness*, **die Anmut** *grace*, **die Großmut** *generosity*. But
the viler qualities remain *masculine*: **der Kleinmut** *cowardice*, **der
Unmut, der Mißmut** *ill-temper*, **der Hochmut, der Übermut** *haughtiness*.
It is best to memorize the gender of each noun as it is met. What is
given above is merely a series of rough pointers to the gender of
German nouns. Declension often depends upon gender, hence the
latter is important.

DECLENSION OF NOUNS

The beginner should take this gently, and avoid mental indigestion,
which will inevitably trouble him if he attempts to memorize too
quickly the immediately following pages. Let him read them through
a few times in order to grasp the general principles of the German
declensions: and return to them later, mastering them a little at a
time. He should, however, refer to them continually while learning
the list of essential nouns on pages 71–107.

Ten Golden Rules

1. In the plural of *all* nouns *all* cases are the same, excepting the dative,
which nearly always ends in **n**.

2. *All* cases of the singular of feminine nouns are the same.
3. Most *monosyllables* with the vowels **a, o, u** and the diphthong **au**, modify them into **ä, ö, ü, äu**, in the plural.
4. The genitive singular of *all* neuter nouns, and of most masculines, excepting those ending in **-e**, ends in **-es**, or **-s**.
5. The accusative singular of *all* neuters and of most masculines except those ending in **-e** is the same as the nominative.
6. Most masculine nouns with nominative ending in **-e** add **-n** for *all* other inflexions, singular and plural.
7. Masculine and neuter nouns ending in **-el, -er, -en** and the diminutive endings **-chen** and **-lcin** add **-s** in the genitive singular and the first two add **-n** in the dative plural. They have no other inflections, but often modify **a, o, u, au** into **ä, ö, ü, äu**, in the plural.
8. Foreign nouns usually follow the rules for pure German nouns, but those not assimilated are irregular in that they follow the rules of their own language.
9. In *all* compound nouns only the final component is declined.
10. Proper names add **-s** in the genitive singular, otherwise do not change.

These rules are 'golden', because the exceptions to them are comparatively rare.

Model for the First Declension

1 (a) Plural *not* modified	1 (b) Plural modified

Masculine

	der Onkel *uncle*		der Apfel *apple*	
	Singular	*Plural*	*Singular*	*Plural*
N	der Onkel	die Onkel	der Apfel	die Äpfel
G	des Onkels	der Onkel	des Apfels	der Äpfel
D	dem Onkel	den Onkeln	dem Apfel	den Äpfeln
A	den Onkel	die Onkel	den Apfel	die Äpfel

Feminine

			die Mutter *mother*	
N	—	—	die Mutter	die Mütter
G	—	—	der Mutter	der Mütter
D	—	—	der Mutter	den Müttern
A	—	—	die Mutter	die Mütter

Neuter

	das Fenster *window*		das Kloster *monastery*	
N	das Fenster	die Fenster	das Kloster	die Klöster
G	des Fensters	der Fenster	des Klosters	der Klöster
D	dem Fenster	den Fenstern	dem Kloster	den Klöstern
A	das Fenster	die Fenster	das Kloster	die Klöster

Like **Onkel** are declined:

Many masculine nouns ending in **-el, -en, -er** (e.g. der **Enkel** *grandson*, der **Rücken** *back*, der **Arbeiter** *workman*).
Also **der Käse** *cheese*.

Like **Apfel** are declined:

The remaining masculine nouns ending in **-el, -en, -er** (e.g. der **Mantel** *coat*, der **Ofen** *stove*, der **Bruder** *brother*).
Like **Mutter**: die **Tochter** *daughter*.

Like **Fenster** are declined:

Most neuter nouns ending in **-el, -en, -er, -chen, -lein**, and words beginning with **Ge-** and ending in **-e** (e.g. das **Mittel** *means*, das **Zeichen** *sign*, das **Zimmer** *room*, das **Mädchen** *girl*, das **Fräulein** *young lady*, das **Gebäude** *building*).

Model for the Second Declension

2 (a) Plural *not* modified   2 (b) Plural modified

Masculine

	der Tag *day*		der Sohn *son*	
	Singular	*Plural*	*Singular*	*Plural*
N	der Tag	die Tage	der Sohn	die Söhne
G	des Tag(e)s	der Tage	des Sohn(e)s	der Söhne
D	dem Tag(e)	den Tagen	dem Sohn(e)	den Söhnen
A	den Tag	die Tage	den Sohn	die Söhne

Feminine

	die Trübsal *affliction*		die Hand *hand*	
N	die Trübsal	die Trübsale	die Hand	die Hände
G	der Trübsal	der Trübsale	der Hand	der Hände
D	der Trübsal	den Trübsalen	der Hand	den Händen
A	die Trübsal	die Trübsale	die Hand	die Hände

Neuter

	das Tier *animal*			das Floß *raft*	
N	das Tier	die Tiere		das Floß	die Flöße
G	des Tier(e)s	der Tiere		des Floßes	der Flöße
D	dem Tier(e)	den Tieren		dem Floß(e)	den Flößen
A	das Tier	die Tiere		das Floß	die Flöße

In this declension are:

Most masculine nouns of one syllable; most masculine nouns ending in **-ig**, **-ich**, **-ing**; masculine nouns borrowed from foreign languages and ending in **-al**, **-at**, **-an**, **-ar**, **-ast**, **-ier**.

Many neuter nouns of one syllable; neuter nouns ending in **-nis**,[1] **-sal**.

Many nouns beginning with **Ge-**.

Most feminine monosyllables.

Model for the Third Declension

	3 (a) Plural *not* modified		3 (b) Plural modified	

Masculine

	der Geist *spirit, mind*			der Wald *forest, wood*	
	Singular	*Plural*		*Singular*	*Plural*
N	der Geist	die Geister		der Wald	die Wälder
G	des Geistes	der Geister		des Wald(e)s	der Wälder
D	dem Geist(e)	den Geistern		dem Wald(e)	den Wäldern
A	den Geist	die Geister		den Wald	die Wälder

Neuter

	das Kind *child*			das Haus *house*	
N	das Kind	die Kinder		das Haus	die Häuser
G	des Kind(e)s	der Kinder		des Hauses	der Häuser
D	dem Kind(e)	den Kindern		dem Haus(e)	den Häusern
A	das Kind	die Kinder		das Haus	die Häuser

This declension includes many nouns of one syllable, nouns ending in **-tum**, a few masculine nouns of one syllable. All nouns in this declension modify vowels **a**, **o**, **u**, **au** in the plural.

[1] Nouns ending in -nis double the final s in the plural:

das Geheimnis *secret*—**die Geheimnisse** *secrets*
die Kenntnis *knowledge*—**die Kenntnisse** *knowledge*

Model for the Fourth Declension

	Masculine der Doktor *doctor*		Feminine die Frau *woman*	
N	der Doktor	die Doktoren	die Frau	die Frauen
G	des Doktors	der Doktoren	der Frau	der Frauen
D	dem Doktor	den Doktoren	der Frau	den Frauen
A	den Doktor	die Doktoren	die Frau	die Frauen

	Neuter das Hemd *shirt*	
N	das Hemd	die Hemden
G	des Hemd(e)s	der Hemden
D	dem Hemd(e)	den Hemden
A	das Hemd	die Hemden

Like **Doktor** are declined:

A few masculine nouns, such as **der Staat** *state*, **der See** *lake*, **der Professor** *professor*, **der Zins** *interest*, **der Muskel** *muscle*.

Like **Frau** are declined:

most feminine nouns of more than one syllable and several monosyllables.

Like **Hemd** are declined:

A few neuter nouns, such as **das Bett** *bed*, **das Ende** *end*, **das Auge** *eye*, **das Leid** *grief*, **das Ohr** *ear*.

Model for the Fifth Declension

	Masculine der Mensch *human being, person*	
N	der Mensch	die Menschen
G	des Menschen	der Menschen
D	dem Menschen	den Menschen
A	den Menschen	die Menschen

Like **Mensch** are declined:

Many masculine nouns ending in **-e** and a few others such as **der Student** *student*, **der Prinz** *prince*, **der Held** *hero*, **der Soldat** *soldier*.

Such nouns are called 'weak nouns' and are listed in the Essential Vocabulary List as such: **der Mensch (-en) (w.n.)**.

The word **der Herr** *Mr., gentleman, master* is unusual and declines as follows:

N	der Herr	die Herren
G	des Herrn	der Herren
D	dem Herrn	den Herren
A	den Herrn	die Herren

Model for the Sixth Declension

Masculine		Neuter	
der Name *name*		**das Herz** *heart*	
N der Name	die Namen	das Herz	die Herzen
G des Namens	der Namen	des Herzens	der Herzen
D dem Namen	den Namen	dem Herzen	den Herzen
A den Namen	die Namen	das Herz	die Herzen

Like **Name** are declined:

A few masculine nouns, such as **der Friede(n)** *peace*, **der Glaube** *belief*, **der Wille** *will*, **der Gedanke** *thought*, **der Haufe(n)** *heap, crowd*, **der Funke(n)** *spark*, **der Same(n)** *seed*.

These nouns are very similar to the weak nouns listed under the fifth declension. They differ only in the genitive singular ending (**-ns**) and in the neuter accusative (no ending).

ADJECTIVES

DECLENSION

1. Adjectives used *alone* after a verb, to describe a state or quality, are invariable: **Er ist gut, sie ist gut, es ist gut.** *He, she, it is good.* Otherwise they are inflected.

2. When preceded by the definite article **(der, die, das)** or by **dieser, jener, jeder, mancher, welcher, derselbe,** the adjective (or adjectives) take the following terminations:

	Masc.	Fem.	Neuter	Plural all genders
N	-e	-e	-e	
G	-en	-en	-en	-en
D	-en	-en	-en	
A	-en	-e	-e	

dem guten Kinde *to the good child*
des guten Vaters *of the good father*
dieser schönen Blumen *of these nice flowers*
jene guten Männer *those good men*

3. When preceded by the indefinite article **(ein, eine, ein)** or by its negation **kein, keine, kein** *no*, or by any of the possessive adjectives (see below), the full inflexions are:

	Masc.	Fem.	Neuter	Plural all genders
N	-er	-e	-es	
G	-en	-en	-en	-en
D	-en	-en	-en	
A	-en	-e	-es	

4. When the adjective is used before a noun, and is not preceded by any of the above, it is declined like **dieser**, except that in the genitive singular of the masculine and neuter the ending **-en** usually takes the place of **-es**, though the latter may be used:

N	**guter alter Wein**	
G	**guten alten Weines**	Plural
D	**gutem altem Wein**	**gute alte Weine,**
A	**guten alten Wein**	etc.

When two or more adjectives precede a noun, both follow the rules given in 2, 3, and 4 above.

Adjectives may often be used as nouns: **der Alte** *the old man*, **ein guter Alter**. Such nouns are listed in the Essential Vocabulary as 'adjectival nouns', e.g. **der Fremde** (a.n.) *stranger.*

Adjectives ending **-el** and **-en** (but not **-er**) usually drop the **-e** in inflexions: **edel** *noble*, **der edle Mann** *the noble man.*

Hoch drops **c** before all vowels: **das hohe Haus** *the high house.*

With all numerals except **ein**, adjectives take the endings of **dieser**: **sieben gute alte Männer.**

COMPARISON

To form the comparative add **-(e)r**⎫
To form the superlative add **-(e)st** ⎬ as in English.

Monosyllables modify **a, o, u** into **ä, ö, ü** (but not au).

alt *old*	**älter** *older*	**ältest** *oldest*
lang *long*	**länger** *longer*	**längst** *longest*
laut *loud*	**lauter** *louder*	**lautest** *loudest*

Comparatives and superlatives are declined like other adjectives.

Than—expressed by **als**: Er ist größer **als** ich. He is bigger *than* I am.

as . . . as: Er ist **so** groß **wie** ich. He is *as* tall *as* I am.

not so . . . as: Er ist **nicht so** groß **wie** ich.

Mehr, weniger, besser . . . als *more, less, better . . . than*

IRREGULAR COMPARISON

The following are of frequent occurrence and should be known:

Positive	*Comparative*		*Superlative*
gut *good*	**besser** *better*		**beste** *the best*
hoch *high*	**höher** *higher*	**der**	**höchste** *the highest*
nahe *near*	**näher** *nearer*	**die**	**nächste** *the nearest, next*
groß *big*	**größer** *bigger*	**das**	**größte** *the biggest*
viel *much*	**mehr** *more*		**meiste** *the most*

POSSESSIVE ADJECTIVES

mein	*my*		**unser**	*our*
dein	*your* (familiar singular)		**euer**	*your* (familiar plural)
sein	*his*, *its* (masc. & neut.)		**Ihr**	*your* (polite, singular, or plural)
ihr	*her*, *its* (fem.)		**ihr**	*their*

The possessive adjectives are declined like **ein** and **kein** (see page 12).

INDEFINITE ADJECTIVES

Note the following adjectives, their meanings, their endings and the endings of the adjectives following them:

alle *all*	alle neuen Arbeiter	*all (the) new workmen*
viele *many*	viele neue Arbeiter	*many new workmen*
mehrere *several*	mehrere neue Autos	*several new cars*
einige *some*	einige reiche Männer	*some rich men*
wenige *few*	wenige deutsche Zeitungen	*few German newspapers*

These adjectives are nearly always found in the plural form.

NUMBERS

CARDINALS

1 ein, eins		**18** achtzehn	
2 zwei		**19** neunzehn	
3 drei		**20** zwanzig	
4 vier		**21** einundzwanzig	
5 fünf		**30** dreißig	
6 sechs		**40** vierzig	
7 sieben		**50** fünfzig	
8 acht		**60** sechzig	
9 neun		**70** siebzig	
10 zehn		**80** achtzig	
11 elf		**90** neunzig	
12 zwölf		**100** hundert	
13 dreizehn		**101** hundert(und)eins	
14 vierzehn		**122** hundertzweiundzwanzig	
15 fünfzehn		**200** zweihundert	
16 sechzehn		**1,000** tausend	
17 siebzehn		**10,000** zehntausend	
		1,000,000 eine Million	
		1,000,000,000 eine Milliarde	

The word **eins** is used only if not followed by another number: **zweihunderteins**. **Zwei** and **drei** have genitives, **zweier, dreier**. All other cardinal numbers are indeclinable. **Hundert** and **tausend** used as nouns take **-e** in nominative plural and **-en** in dative plural: **hunderte von Menschen** *hundreds of people*.

ORDINALS

Ordinals are formed from cardinals by adding **-t** from 2 to 19, and **-st** from 20 upwards: **der zweite** *the second*, **der dreißigste** *the thirtieth*, **der hundertste** *the hundredth*, **der vierundzwanzigste** *the twenty-fourth*, etc. They are written with a full stop after the number: **Der 1. Januar**, *1st of January*.

Irregulars: **der erste** *the first*, **der dritte** *the third*, **der siebte** *the seventh*, **der achte** *the eighth*.

Ordinals are declined like ordinary adjectives, but only the last number of a compound is inflected: **der fünfzehnhundertneunundzwanzigste**.

Miscellaneous

In German fractions are written with a comma and full numbers with a full stop: 6,25 (English 6·25) and 1.000 (English 1,000).

ein Drittel (*n.*) *a third*, **ein Zwanzigstel** (*n.*) *a twentieth part*, **ein Viertel** (*n.*) *a fourth*, **ein Hundertstel** (*n.*) *a hundredth part*, etc.

These are formed from the ordinals with the suffix **-el**.

anderthalb, *one and a half*, **zweieinhalb** *two and a half*, etc., **halb**, *half*, **die Hälfte** *half*.

einfach *simple*, **zweifach**, **doppelt** *double*, **dreifach** *threefold*, *etc.*; **einerlei** *of one kind*, **zweierlei** *of two kinds*, **dreierlei**, etc., are indeclinable.

einzeln *individual*, *separate*; **der einzelne Deutsche** *the individual German*.

einzig *single*, *only;* **kein einziger Mann** *not a single man*.

einmal *once*, **zweimal** *twice*, **dreimal** *three times*, etc.

erstens *in the first place*, **zweitens** *secondly*, **drittens**, etc.; **zuerst** *at first*.

Different Usage in German

Some nouns denoting weight and measure are put in the singular: **drei Glas Wasser** *three glasses of water*, **sieben Fuß hoch** *seven feet high*.

Wie spät ist es? *What time is it?*
Es ist ein, zwei, drei Uhr. *It is one, two, three o'clock.*
Es ist zwanzig Minuten nach sechs. *It is 6.20.*
Es ist viertel nach zwei.⎱
Es ist viertel drei.⎰ *It is a quarter-past two.*
Es ist halb drei. *It is half-past two.*
Es ist dreiviertel drei. *It is a quarter to three.*
Den wievielten haben wir heute? Den dritten. Den siebten. *What is the date? The third. The seventh.*
vor acht Tagen *a week ago.*
in vierzehn Tagen *in a fortnight's time.*
im Jahre neunzehnhundertachtundsechzig *in (the year) 1968.*

PRONOUNS

In German *it* takes the gender of the noun to which it refers:

Wo ist **das** Mädchen? Where is the girl?
Es ist hier. *She* is here.

Wo ist **mein** Stock? Where is my stick?
Er ist nicht hier. *It* is not here.

Haben Sie **die** Blume? Have you the flower?
Ja, ich habe **sie**. Yes, I have *it*.

Note the idiomatic usage:

Wer ist es? *Who is it?*
Ich bin es. *It's me.*
Waren Sie es? *Was it you?*
Ja, ich war es. *Yes, it was me.*
Er ist müde und seine Schwester ist es auch. *He is tired and so is his sister.*
Es war einmal ein Mann. *There was once a man.*

The dative and accusative of **es** is formed by **da-** (**dar-** before vowels) with certain prepositions, and compounded with them:

davon *of it, from it*	**darin** *in it, therein*
damit *with it*	**daraus** *out of it*

REFLEXIVE PRONOUNS

The accusatives and datives of the first and second persons in the table of personal pronouns are used as reflexive pronouns—that is, when it is necessary to refer back an action to the subject (nominative) of the sentence:

He killed himself: *himself* is a reflexive pronoun.
I wash myself: *myself* „ „ „ „

The word **sich** is used for all genders, singular and plural, accusative *and* dative, of the third person, and also as reflexive for **Sie**, *you*.

Examples:

Ich wasche mich (acc.).	but	**Ich wasche mir** (*dat.*) **die Hände.**
I wash (*myself*).		*I wash my hands.*
Er wäscht sich (acc.).	but	**Er wäscht sich** (dat.) **die Hände.**
He washes (*himself*).		*He washes his hands.*
Sie irren sich.		*You err* (*to yourself*); *you are mistaken.*

The word **selbst** *self* is used to emphasize any of the personal pronouns, and must not be confused with the reflexives:

Ich selbst *I myself*	**Sie selbst** *you yourself*
Er hat es selbst getan.	*He did it himself.*

Before a noun **selbst** has the meaning *even*:

Selbst seine Mutter liebt ihn nicht. *Even his mother does not love him.*

A Table of Personal Pronouns

Person	Nominative	Genitive	Dative	Accusative
1.	ich, *I*	meiner, *of me*	mir, *to me*	mich, *me*
2.	du, *you* (*thou*)[1]	deiner, *of you* (*thee*)	dir, *to you* (*thee*)	dich, *you* (*thee*)
3.	er, *he, it*	seiner, *of him, it*	ihm, *to him, it*	ihn, *him, it*
	sie, *she, it*	ihrer, *of her, it*	ihr, *to her, it*	sie, *her, it*
	es, *it*	seiner, *of it*	ihm, *to it*	es, *it*
Plural				
1.	wir, *we*	unser, *of us*	uns, *to us*	uns, *us*
2.	ihr, *you*[1] (*ye*)	euer, *of you*	euch, *to you* (*ye*)	euch, *you* (*ye*)
3.	sie, *they*	ihrer, *of them*	ihnen, *to them*	sie, *them*
Note:	Sie, *you*	Ihrer, *of you*	Ihnen, *to you*	Sie, *you*

[1] English *you* can be translated in three ways: By **du** when speaking to a deity, intimate friends, relations, children, or animals. **Ihr** is the plural of **du**, and is used also in poetry, sermons, and other solemn or heavy discourses. **Sie** is the ordinary word for *you*, and should always be used until the language and people are well known. It is written with a capital (**Sie**) to distinguish it from **sie**, they, but takes the same form of the verb: **Sie haben** *you have:* **sie haben** *they have,* etc.

RELATIVE PRONOUNS

A relative pronoun is one which connects the noun or pronoun to which it refers with the part of the sentence which follows. Thus: The man *whom* I know. The house *that* Jack built. *Whom* and *that* are relative pronouns. In English the relative is often omitted as: *The house Jack built;* which would be quite as correct as: *The house that Jack built*—and would probably be used in conversation.

In German relatives may *never* be omitted, so if you wish to say, 'The woman I saw with you to-day,' it must be **Die Frau, die ich heute mit Ihnen sah.**

There are two main relatives in German: **der, die, das** and **welcher, welche, welches.**[1] Their declension must be specially learnt, as it is slightly irregular.

	Masc.	Fem.	Neuter	Plural of all genders
N	der	die	das	die
G	dessen	deren	dessen	deren
D	dem	der	dem	denen
A	den	die	das	die
N	welcher	welche	welches	welche
	(No genitive. Use:			
G	dessen	deren	dessen	deren)
D	welchem	welcher	welchem	welchen
A	welchen	welche	welches	welche

Agreement

The relative agrees in gender and number with the noun to which it refers. Thus:

> **der Mann, der** (or **welcher**) . . . *the man who . . .*
> **die Frau, die** (or **welche**) . . . *the woman who . . .*
> **das Kind, das** (or **welches**) . . . *the child who . . .*

But the relative takes its case from its own clause:

> **Die Frau, deren Buch verloren ist.** *The woman whose book is lost.*

[1] In speaking *always* use der, die, das.

Word-order

It will be seen in the last example that the word order differs from English. The rule is that, in the part of a sentence introduced by a relative pronoun, the verb is placed at the end, with past participle or infinitive before auxiliary. Hence:

Der Mann, welcher den Garten gekauft hat. *The man who has bought the garden.*

The whole question of word-order will, however, be treated later (see page 63).

Contraction with prepositions

Wo (wor before a vowel) is used with prepositions for both the above relatives, when the clause preceding is not a personal one:

Das Haus, worin (or **in dem** or **in welchem**) **ich wohne, ist sehr warm.** *The house in which (wherein) I live is very warm.*

Other contractions are:

woran	*at which, what*	**worauf**	*upon which, that*
woraus	*from which*	**wobei**	*at, near which*
wodurch	*through, by which*	**wofür**	*for which*
worin	*in which*	**womit**	*with which*
worüber	*over which*	**worunter**	*under, among which*
wovon	*of which*	**wozu**	*to which*

All these words are also used as interrogatives.

Was is usually used as the relative pronoun after

alles	*everything*	**nichts**	*nothing*
das Erste	*the first*	**das Letzte**	*the last*
das Beste	*the best*		

alles, was Sie sagten . . . *everything you said* . . .
das Beste, was Sie haben . . . *the best you have* . . .

INTERROGATIVES

These are the pronouns which ask questions:

Who goes there?	*What* are you doing?	*Which* one do you prefer?
wer? *who?*	**was?** *what?*	**welche-?** *which one(s)?*

Who, what, which, are interrogative pronouns.

N	wer? *who?*	was? *what?*
G	wessen? *whose?*	wessen? *of what?*
D	wem? *to whom?*	wo(r) + prep? *to what?*
A	wen? *whom?*	was? *what?*

A useful interrogative is: **Was für ein . . .?** *What sort of a . . .?*
The **ein** is declined in the ordinary manner:

Was für ein Mann ist Ihr Vater? *What sort of a man is your father?*
Was für Leute sind es? *What kind of people are they?*

Contractions

Was? *What?* preceded by a preposition is contracted as explained on page 30:

Wovon sprechen Sie? *What are you speaking about?*

Of which, when it is *not* possessive, is translated by **von** with the dative:

Von welchen dieser Bücher sprachen Sie? *Which of these books were you talking about?*

DEMONSTRATIVES

These are both adjectives and pronouns which point out or demonstrate. The demonstratives already encountered (see page 10) are:

dieser *this (one),* also used for *the latter,*
jener *that (one),* also used for *the former*

In modern conversational German *this one* and *that one* are often expressed by **dieser** and **der:**

Dieser (hier) ist neu aber **der** (da) ist alt. *This one is new but that one is old.*
Diese Dame kennt mich aber **die** Dame kennt mich nicht. *This lady knows me but that lady does not know me.*

dies and **das,** *this* and *that:*

Dies ist gut. *This is good.*   **Das** ist schlecht. *That is bad.*

The contractions **da(r)**+preposition listed on page 27 are also used to express *this* and *that*:

darin *in that* (*this*)   **daraus** *out of this* (*that*)
darüber *over this* (*that*)   **davon** *of/from this* (*that*)

Other demonstratives are: **Der(jenige), die(jenige), das(jenige).**

Mein Hut und **der(jenige)** meines Freundes. My hat and *that* of my friend.

Note also: **derselbe, dieselbe, dasselbe** *the same*
          der andere, die andere, das andere *the other*

Such a followed by a noun is **solcher, solche, solches**:

ein **solcher** Mann, eine **solche** Frau, ein **solches** Kind *such a man, woman, child*

Such a followed by an adjective is **so**:

ein **so** kleines Kind *such a small child*

POSSESSIVE PRONOUNS

The possessive pronouns are formed from the possessive adjectives listed on page 24 and declined like **dieser** (page 11):

Wessen Hut ist das? Es ist meiner. *Whose hat is this? It's mine*
Ist dieses Auto dein(e)s? *Is this car yours?*

Gehören, *to belong*, is the most common way of denoting ownership:

Dieser Hut gehört mir. *This hat is mine* (*belongs to me*).
Diese Häuser gehören uns. *These houses are ours.*

INDEFINITE PRONOUNS

There is a group of words which may conveniently be called indefinite pronouns. They occur very frequently and should be known thoroughly:

Man expresses *one, they, people* (cf. French *on*):

Man sagt . . . *They say . . .*
Wenn man müde ist . . . *When you are tired . . .*

Man is also often used where English would use the passive voice:

> Hier spricht man deutsch. *German is spoken here.*
> Man hat mich eingeladen. *I have been invited* (lit: One has invited me).

einander	*one another*	Sie küßten einander.	*They kissed each other.*
selbst	*self*	Ich habe es selbst getan.	*I did it myself.*
niemand	*no one*	Niemand hilft mir.	*No one helps me.*
etwas	*something*	Ich gebe dir etwas.	*I'll give you something.*
all	*all*	All meine Häuser.	*All my houses.*
jemand	*someone, anyone*	Hat jemand hier ein Wörterbuch?	*Has anyone here a dictionary?*
jedermann	*everyone*	Jedermann kennt ihn.	*Everyone knows him.*

VERBS

The German verb may appear formidable, but it is by no means as bad as it looks. The student will soon find that very often it greatly resembles the English verb. It is not essential to know every form, every subtlety and idiomatic usage. But what follows in these pages (unless expressly stated to be for reference only) should be mastered. Mastery may be recognized when that part of a verb required to state an idea comes to the mind without hesitation.

PARTS OF THE VERB WHICH MUST BE KNOWN

For practical purposes the parts of the German verb required are:
1. Infinitive: 'that part of a verb which names the action, without reference to the doer, and is therefore not limited by person or by number.' Thus **loben** *to praise*, **essen** *to eat*, **schreiben** *to write*.
2. Present tense indicative: corresponds to the three English forms, *I speak*, *I do speak*, *I am speaking*, all of which are translated by one form in German: **ich spreche**. Similarly, **ich lobe** *I praise*, *I do praise*, *I am praising*, etc.
3. Simple past tense indicative (also called the imperfect): corresponds to the English, *I (have) praised*, *I was praising*, *I did praise*, etc., all of which are represented in German by one form: **ich lobte**.
4. Simple future indicative: corresponds to the English, *I shall praise*, etc., and is formed in German with the auxiliary **werden**: **ich werde loben** *I shall praise*.
5. Past participle: is used to form compound tenses, and sometimes as an adjective: *I have praised, sung, spoken* **ich habe gelobt, gesungen, gesprochen**. (**Gelobt, gesungen, gesprochen** are past participles.)

If the infinitive, the imperfect, and the past participle are known, *all* other parts can be formed by the 'Ten Golden Rules' on page 36.

CLASSIFICATION OF VERBS, ETC.

All infinitives of German verbs end in -en or -n. That part of a verb which remains when we cut off this -en or -n is called the 'root'.

All parts of a verb consist of this root plus an ending or inflexion: **ich lob-e** *I praise*, **ich lob-te** *I praised*. **Lob-** is the root, **-e** and **-te** are endings. In addition to the ending, nearly all past participles have a prefix **ge-**: **ge-lob-t** *praised*.

Verbs are said to be regular (or 'weak') when, like **loben**, the past tense is formed by adding **-te** (or **-ete**) to the root, and by prefixing **ge-** and adding **-t** to the root to form the past participle.

Verbs are said to be irregular (or 'strong') when the root vowel in the past differs from that of the infinitive: **geben** *to give* (root, **geb-**), imperfect, **ich gab**. (Note the English: *to give, I gave*.)

The past participle of strong verbs is usually formed by prefixing **ge-** and adding the ending **-en**, but the vowel may differ from that of the root of the infinitive: **singen** *to sing*; imperfect, **ich sang** *I sang*; past participle, **gesungen** *sung*. **Sprechen** *to speak;* **ich sprach** *I spoke;* **ich habe gesprochen** *I have spoken*.

Those are examples of strong verbs. Also: **tragen** *to carry, to wear;* **ich trug** *I wore;* **ich habe getragen** *I have worn*. Here, **getragen** retains the root vowel of the infinitive.

The strong or irregular verbs are best mastered in groups, in accordance with the changes of the root vowels. We shall come to them later (see pages 45–50).

The present participle of all verbs ends **-end**, corresponding to English **-ing**, and it is very often used as an adjective: **loben** *to praise*, **lobend** *praising;* **lieben** *to love*, **liebend** *loving*, **eine liebende Mutter** *a loving mother*. It is also sometimes used as a noun: **reisen** *to travel*, **reisend** *travelling*, **der Reisende** *the traveller* (but **ein Reisender**). And as an adverb: **lachen** *to laugh*, **lachend** *laughing*, **lachend sagte ich ...** *laughingly (or laughing) I said ...*

AUXILIARY VERBS

Auxiliary verbs are so called because not only are they used alone in their original meanings, but as helps to form the compound tenses of *all* other verbs. They are the most frequently recurring verbs in the language and must be known thoroughly.

In German there are three simple auxiliaries: **haben** *to have*, **sein** *to be*, **werden** *to become*. They are conjugated in the table on page 40. **Haben** is an example of a weak verb; **sein** of one that is irregular; and **werden** of a straightforward strong verb. In English we always use *to have* in the formation of compound tenses but in German many verbs take **sein**, as will be seen later.

TO FORM THE TENSES OF ALL REGULAR OR WEAK VERBS

The verb **loben** in the table on page 40 is given as a model of a fully conjugated regular or weak verb. It is given for reference and practice. All regular verbs—that is, *verbs not given with the 'strongs' and irregulars below*—follow the model of **loben**. All tenses of regular verbs can be formed by following these rules:

TEN GOLDEN RULES FOR REGULAR VERBS

1. Verbs with roots ending in **-d, -t, -tm, -chn, -ckn, -dn, -fn, -gn,** retain **e** of the infinitive throughout. Verbs with roots ending **-s, -z, -sch**, retain this **e** only in the second person of the present indicative:

> **antworten** *to answer*   ich antworte, du antwortest, er antwortet *I answer*, etc.
> ich antwortete *I answered*, etc.

Similarly, **regnen** *to rain*, **öffnen** *to open*, **baden** *to bathe*, etc.

2. To form the present tense indicative: drop **-en** of the infinitive (i.e. find the root) and add **-e, -st, -t, -en, -t, -en (ich lobe,** etc.).

3. The imperfect indicative is formed by adding to the root: **-te, -test, -te, -ten, -tet, -ten (ich lobte,** etc.).

4. To form the future: use the present of **werden** with the infinitive of the verb of which the future is required (**ich werde loben,** etc.). This applies to *all* verbs, regular and irregular.

5. To form the conditional: use imperfect subjunctive of **werden** with the infinitive (**ich würde loben** *I should praise*, etc.). This applies to *all* verbs, regular and irregular.

6. To form the present subjunctive: add to the root **-e, -est, -e, -en, -et, -en (ich lobe, du lobest, er lobe,** etc.).

7. The imperfect subjunctive is the same as the imperfect indicative (**ich lobte**, etc.). In strong verbs there is usually modification of the vowel (**ich sänge**).

8. To form the imperative: add the pronoun **Sie** to the infinitive form (**Loben Sie!** *Praise!*). This works only for the second person plural, which is the one most frequently used.

9. All verbs ending in **-ieren** are regular. They require no **ge-** in the past participle:

regieren *to rule*	**regiert**
marschieren *to march*	**marschiert**
studieren *to study*	**studiert**

10. Verbs ending **-eln, -ern**, drop **e** before **l** and **r** in the first person singular of the present tense:

handeln *to treat, act.* **ich handle** *I act*

THE SUBJUNCTIVE MOOD

In most grammars the subjunctive mood is given a position of importance and, for fine shades of meaning, it is very necessary. The student who wishes to know his German thoroughly cannot afford to neglect it. But it is not *essential* for the expression of the common ideas of everyday life. One should, however, be able to recognize it. it is usually formed as follows:

Present subjunctive: add to the root **-e, -est, -e, -en, -et, -en.**

ich habe	wir haben
du habest	ihr habet
er habe	sie haben

(**ich lobe, ich werde, ich singe,** etc.)
The past or imperfect is the same as that of the indicative (i.e. given in the table on page 40), but usually **a, o, u** become **ä, ö, ü,** and **-e** is added to the singular:

ich spräche	ich könnte (from **können** *to be able*)
ich würde	ich trüge (from **tragen** *to bear, carry*)
ich wäre	

The subjunctive is used mainly in indirect speech.

THE IMPERATIVE, OR HOW TO GIVE COMMANDS

This is formed by placing the pronoun after the plural of the present tense:

Loben Sie ihn! *Praise him!*   **Gehen wir.** *Let us go.*

It may also be formed with the verb **lassen** *to let, allow*:

Lassen Sie uns kaufen! *Let us buy.*
Lassen Sie uns heraus(gehen)! *Let us (get) out of here.*
Lassen Sie ihn kommen! *Let him come.*

TO USE THE VERB INTERROGATIVELY

Merely put the personal pronoun after:

Haben Sie einen Hut? *Have you a hat?*
Rauchen Sie? *Do you smoke?*
Spricht er? *Does he speak?*
Sind Sie müde? *Are you tired?*
Was sagten Sie? *What did you say?*

Similarly the noun, with all attributes, is put after the verb:

Ist meine Schwester zu Hause? *Is my sister at home?*

THE NEGATIVE OF VERBS

Use the word **nicht** *not*. In simple tenses, direct statements, it is placed immediately after the verb:

Ich lobe nicht. *I do not praise.*
Ich spreche nicht. *I am not speaking.*

In compound tenses always *before* infinitives or past participles.
   Otherwise **nicht** stands *after* a direct object, an adverb of time, or *before* an adverb of place or manner, a preposition, or an emphatic word.

Ich habe ihn nicht gefunden. *I have not found him.*
Ich will nicht sagen. *I will not say.*

Ich gab ihm den Wein nicht. *I did not give him the wine.*
Er ist nicht hier. *He is not here.*
Er ist nicht mit uns gekommen. *He has not come with us.*

TO FORM THE PASSIVE OF VERBS

The passive of all verbs is formed with **werden**. Thus:

Ich werde gelobt. *I am praised* (or *being praised*).
Ich wurde gelobt. *I was praised.*
Ich werde gelobt werden. *I shall be praised.*

The past participle of **werden** used in this sense is **worden**:

Ich bin gelobt worden (not geworden). *I have been praised.*

Note: **man** is often used instead of the passive form (see page 32).

REFLEXIVE VERBS

A reflexive verb is one in which the action performed is suffered by
the subject. Thus: I wash myself. In German there are many verbs
which are reflexive—that is, they are conjugated with two pronouns
instead of one:

sich freuen *to be glad*
ich freue mich   wir freuen uns
du freust dich   ihr freut euch
er freut sich   sie freuen sich

Imperfect: **ich freute mich.**   Future: **ich werde mich freuen.**
Imperative: **Freuen Sie sich!** *Be glad!*
Note: All reflexive verbs in German are conjugated with **haben**:

Ich habe mich gefreut *I have been glad* (*was glad*).

Examples of reflexive verbs: **sich irren** *to make a mistake,* **sich erinnern** *to remember,* (but **erinnern** *to remind*).

Table of auxiliaries and the weak verb loben

	haben, *to have*	sein, *to be*	werden, *to become*	loben, *to praise*
1.	haben, *to have*	sein, *to be*	werden, *to become*	loben, *to praise*
2.	habend, *having*	seiend, *being*	werdend, *becoming*	lobend, *praising*
3.	gehabt, *had*	gewesen, *been*	geworden, *become*	gelobt, *praised*
4.	ich habe, *I have* du hast er, sie, es hat wir haben ihr habt sie haben	ich bin, *I am* du bist er ist wir sind ihr seid sie sind	ich werde, *I become* du wirst er wird wir werden ihr werdet sie werden	ich lobe, *I praise* du lobst er lobt wir loben ihr lob(e)t sie loben
5.	ich hatte, *I had* du hattest er hatte wir hatten ihr hattet sie hatten	ich war, *I was* du warst er war wir waren ihr wart wie waren	ich wurde, *I became* du wurdest er wurde wir wurden ihr wurdet sie wurden	ich lobte, *I praised* du lobtest er lobte wir lobten ihr lobtet sie lobten
6.	ich habe gehabt, *I have had, etc.*	ich bin gewesen, *I have been, etc.*	ich bin geworden, *I have become, etc.*	ich habe gelobt, *I have praised, etc.*
7.	ich hatte gehabt, *I had had, etc.*	ich war gewesen, *I had been, etc.*	ich war geworden, *I had become, etc.*	ich hatte gelobt, *I had praised, etc.*
8.	ich werde haben, *I shall have, etc.*	ich werde sein, *I shall be, etc.*	ich werde werden, *I shall become, etc.*	ich werde loben, *I shall praise, etc.*
9.	ich würde haben, *I would have, etc.*	ich würde sein, *I would be, etc.*	ich würde werden, *I would become, etc.*	ich würde loben, *I would praise, etc.*

In the above Table: 1, is the Infinitive; 2, Present Participle; 3, Past Participle; 4, Present Tense; 5, Past or Imperfect Tense; 6, Perfect Tense; 7, Pluperfect Tense; 8, Future Tense; 9, Conditional.

There are two more tenses: Future Perfect, **ich werde gehabt haben,** *I shall have had;* Past Conditional, **ich würde gehabt haben,** etc. But these are rare.

THE SIX AUXILIARIES OF MOOD

In addition to the three simple auxiliaries **haben, sein,** and **werden,** there are six important verbs called 'auxiliaries of mood', because, although alone they may convey no very definite or complete idea, when used with other verbs they modify the meanings of these other verbs. The six verbs are:

können	**dürfen**
mögen	**müssen**
sollen	**wollen**

As these words recur continually, it is important that their meaning and uses should be fully grasped.

Können, konnte, gekonnt denotes the *power* to do something. It translates all the English words which signify *ability, possibility,* or *likelihood* of doing something. Thus: **Ich kann nicht kommen, schreiben, lesen** *I cannot come, write, read.*

Mögen, mochte, gemocht denotes a *liking* or *preference* to do something, and also a *possibility* (often depending on a wish that it may be so). Thus: **Das mag sein** *That may be.* **Er mochte fünfzig Jahre alt sein** *He might have been fifty years old.*
Note the following usage of **mögen:**

	1. **gern**	
	like to	
Ich möchte	2. **lieber**	**deutsch sprechen.**
I should	*rather (prefer to)*	*speak German.*
	3. **am liebsten**	
	like best to	

Note the two forms: **mochte** means *might have been* or *seemed to be,* but **möchte** means *should like.*
Note also the idiom: **Ich mag ihn (sie) nicht** *I dislike him (her).*

Sollen, sollte, gesollt denotes a *duty* or *obligation,* also a *command.* Thus: **Du sollst nicht stehlen** *Thou shalt not steal.* **Was soll ich tun?** *What shall I do?*

Dürfen, durfte, gedurft: *to be permitted to,* or *to be likely to.* Thus: **Darf ich mitkommen?** *May I come with (you)?* **Sie dürfen es** *You may.* **Sie dürfen hier nicht parken** *You must not park here.* **Das dürfte richtig sein** *That is probably right.*

Müssen, mußte, gemußt corresponds to the English *must*, denoting *compulsion* or *necessity*. Thus: **Er muß gehen, kommen** *He must go, come.* **Sie muß müde sein** *She must be tired.*

Wollen, wollte, gewollt: a vague word this, so one must be wary. Denotes *willingness* or *desire*. Thus: **Wollen Sie mit mir kommen?** *Will you come with me?* **Wollen Sie die Güte haben ...** *Would you be so good as to ...*
Wollen must not be used for simple futures.

Note: A mood auxiliary, in addition to its ordinary past participles given above, also uses its infinitive as past participle—the latter when another infinitive depends upon it: **Er hat nicht gehen können** (instead of **gekonnt**). *He was unable to go.* If there is no second infinitive, the ordinary form is used: **Er hat es nicht gekonnt.** *He has not been able to.* **Zu** is never used after a mood auxiliary before an infinitive.[1]

The so-called 'double infinitive' construction may also occur with the verbs: **fühlen** *to feel*, **helfen** *to help*, **hören** *to hear*, **lassen** *to have* (*sth. done*), **lehren** *to teach*, **lernen** *to learn*, and **sehen** *to see*.

> **Ich habe Sie singen hören.** *I heard you singing.*
> **Er hat mich kommen sehen.** *He saw me coming.*

IRREGULAR PRESENT TENSES

I can	*I may*	*I am allowed to*
ich kann	mag	darf
du kannst	magst	darfst
er kann	mag	darf
wir können	mögen	dürfen
ihr könnt	mögt	dürft
sie können	mögen	dürfen

I must	*I am to*	*I want*
ich muß	soll	will
du mußt	sollst	willst
er muß	soll	will
wir müssen	sollen	wollen
ihr müßt	sollt	wollt
sie müssen	sollen	wollen

[1] **Brauchen** *to use*, *need*, is also used as an auxiliary of mood, but only in the *negative* form: **Er braucht nicht (zu) kommen.** *He need not come.* **Brauchen** in this sense is often followed by **zu**.

IMPERSONAL VERBS

These verbs have **es** *it* as their subject:

> **Es regnet** *It's raining.*
> **Es friert.** *It's freezing.*
> **Es schneit.** *It's snowing.*
> **Es donnert.** *It's thundering.*
> **Es gibt** ... *There is (are)* ...
> **Es ist, sind** ... *There is, are* ...
> **Es tut mir leid.** *I'm sorry.*
> **Es gefällt mir (hier).** *I like it (here).*
> **Es geht mir gut.** *I'm well.*
> **Es fehlt mir (ein Glas).** *I'm short of (a glass).*
> **Es macht nichts.** *It doesn't matter.*
> **Es schmeckt mir.** *I like it (of food or drink).*

SEPARABLE AND INSEPARABLE VERBS

Most German verbs can change or expand their meaning by the addition of prefixes. These prefixes are either *separable* or *inseparable*. By separable is meant that the prefix can be detached from the root verb. Thus: **zurückkommen** *to come back*—**Ich komme zurück** *I come back*.

An inseparable root verb *never* parts with its prefix. Thus: **bekommen** *to get, obtain*—**Ich bekomme** *I obtain*, **Ich habe bekommen** *I have obtained*. And the inseparable prefixes are always *un*accented: **bekomm′en**, etc.

1. Inseparable prefixes: **be-, ge-, ent-, er-, emp-, ver-, zer-, miß-** and **wider-.** This list must be learnt and the simple or original meanings of the prefixes to be found on page 60 should be mastered.

An inseparable verb follows exactly the conjugation of its simple root verb (**ich bekomme, du bekommst, er bekommt,** etc.) but no **ge-** is added to the past participle.

---

[1] Distinguish the inseparable **wider** *against* from the separable **wieder** *again*.

2. Separable prefixes with their original meanings are:

ab- *off*	**hin-** *from one, thither*
an- *on*	**los-** *loose, off*
auf- *up, upon*	**mit-** *with*
aus- *out*	**nach-** *after*
bei- *by*	**nieder-** *down*
da-, dar- *there*	**vor-** *before*
ein- *in, into*	**voran-** *before*
empor- *up*	**weg-** *away*
entgegen- *against, towards*	**weiter-** *further*
entzwei- *in two*	**wieder-** *again*
fort- *away*	**zu-** *to*
gegen- *against*	**zurück-** *back*
her- *towards one, hither*	**zusammen-** *together*

This list is also very important. A separable prefix is accented.

Examples: **schneiden** *to cut*, **abschneiden** *to cut off;* **wiederkommen** *to come again*, **zurückkommen** *to come back;* **her-** and **hin-** can be used either alone or with other prefixes: **hereinkommen.**

The conjugation of these separable verbs follows certain rules:

(i) In the present and past tense (of both indicative and subjunctive) the prefix is despatched to the *end* of the clause: **reisen** *to travel*, **abreisen** *to set out, depart*, **ich reise ab** *I set out*.

(ii) In the infinitive and past participle **zu** (when used) and **ge-** are placed between the prefix and the root verb: **Er wünscht auszugehen.** *He wishes to go out.* **Sie sind zusammengekommen.** *They have come together.*

(iii) In the imperative the prefix is always sent to the end of the clause: **Gehen Sie sofort weg!** *Go away immediately!*

Otherwise the separate verbs are conjugated like their 'root' verbs:

> **wieder(zu)kommen** *to come again.*
> **Ich kam wieder.** *I came again.*
> **Ich bin wiedergekommen.** *I have come again.*
> **Ich werde wiederkommen.** *I will come again.*

3. Separable or inseparable, according to meaning are:

durch *through*	**um** *about* (also indicates change)
hinter *behind*	**unter** *under*
über *over*	**voll** *full*
wieder *again*	

When each part of the verb has its original meaning, the prefix bears the principal accent and is separable: **wieder'holen (ich hole wieder, wieder'geholt)** *to fetch again*, **um'stellen** *to put round*, *to change*.

But when the compound has a *figurative* meaning, the prefix is unaccented and inseparable: **wiederho'len (ich wiederho'le, wiederho'lt)** *to repeat*, **umste'llen** *to encircle*.

WISSEN AND KENNEN

Wissen *to know* denotes knowledge gained by study or learning (French: *savoir*). **Kennen** (French: *connaître*) *to know* indicates an acquaintance with something:

> **Kennen Sie ihn?** *Do you know him?*
> **Wissen Sie, wie er heißt?** *Do you know his name?*
> **Ich kenne den Inhalt des Briefes.** *I am acquainted with the contents of the letter.*
> **Ich weiß nicht, von wem der Brief ist.** *I do not know who the letter is from.*

VERBS CONJUGATED WITH SEIN

Verbs of motion and their compounds are conjugated with **sein**: **gehen** *to go*, **abreisen** *to depart*, etc. Also the verbs **werden** *to become*, **sterben** *to die*, **bleiben** *to stay*, and **sein** itself.

IRREGULAR VERBS

When the student has become thoroughly familiar with the preceding pages, and especially with the 'Ten Golden Rules' for the formation of all tenses, the 'strong' and irregular verbs should be attacked.

The easiest way to learn them is by the groups into which they fall naturally by the changes of the root vowel in the past tense and past participle. Each group should be known before the next is approached. Owing to the familiar 'sound' of many of these verbs, it is surprising how quickly they can be learnt.

In the list which follows only the principal parts of each verb are given—infinitive, past or imperfect tense, and past participle—as from them *all* other parts can be formed by means of the 'Golden Rules'.

Most strong verbs modify root-vowels **a, o, au**, in the second and third persons singular of the present indicative: **ich fahre, du fährst, er fährt**. Nearly all strong verbs with root-vowel **e** in Groups II, IV, and V take **i** or **ie** in the second and third persons singular of the present indicative and the second person singular of the imperative: **ich sterbe, du stirbst, er stirbt**. The second person singular imperative of such verbs does not take the ending **e: stirb!** Werden forms **ich werde, du wirst, er wird**.

Group I

Infinitive	Imperfect	Past Part.	English
ei	**i, ie**	**i, ie**	
beißen[1]	biß	gebissen	*bite*
*bleiben	blieb	geblieben	*remain*
gleichen	glich	geglichen	*be like, equal*
*gleiten	glitt	geglitten	*glide*
greifen	griff	gegriffen	*seize*
leihen	lieh	geliehen	*lend*
reißen	riß	gerissen	*tear*
*scheiden	schied	geschieden	*leave, separate*
scheinen	schien	geschienen	*shine, seem*
schreien	schrie	geschrieen	*cry, shout*
schreiben	schrieb	geschrieben	*write*
schweigen	schwieg	geschwiegen	*be silent*
*steigen	stieg	gestiegen	*mount*
streichen	strich	gestrichen	*stroke, paint*
streiten	stritt	gestritten	*quarrel*
treiben	trieb	getrieben	*drive, force*
leiden	litt	gelitten	*suffer*
schneiden	schnitt	geschnitten	*cut*
weisen	wies	gewiesen	*show, point*
Note:			
heißen	hieß	geheißen	*call, be called*

[1] All in Group I take **i** before **ch, f, ß (ss), t**; otherwise **ie**.
* Verbs marked with an asterisk take **sein** to form their compound tenses.

Group II

Infinitive	Imperfect	Past Part.	English
ie	o	o	
biegen	bog	gebogen	*bend*
bieten	bot	geboten	*bid, offer*
*fliegen	flog	geflogen	*fly*
*fliehen	floh	geflohen	*flee, escape*
*fließen	floß	geflossen	*flow*
genießen	genoß	genossen	*enjoy*
gießen	goß	gegossen	*pour*
riechen	roch	gerochen	*smell, reek*
schieben	schob	geschoben	*shove, push*
schießen	schoß	geschossen	*shoot*
schließen	schloß	geschlossen	*shut, close*
verlieren	verlor	verloren	*lose*
ziehen	zog	gezogen	*draw, move*
lügen	log	gelogen	*tell a lie*
heben	hob	gehoben	*heave, raise, lift*

Group III

Infinitive	Imperfect	Past Part.	English
i	a	u	
binden	band	gebunden	*bind*
finden	fand	gefunden	*find*
*gelingen	gelang	gelungen	*succeed*
klingen	klang	geklungen	*sound (clink)*
*(ver)schwinden	schwand	geschwunden	*disappear*
singen	sang	gesungen	*sing*
*sinken	sank	gesunken	*sink*
*springen	sprang	gesprungen	*spring, jump*
trinken	trank	getrunken	*drink*
zwingen	zwang	gezwungen	*force*

Group IV

Infinitive	Imperfect	Past Part.	English
e	a	o	
befehlen(ie)[1]	befahl	befohlen	*command, order*
brechen(i)	brach	gebrochen	*break*
erschrecken(i)[2]	erschrak	erschrocken	*be frightened*
helfen(i)	half	geholfen	*help*
nehmen(i)[3]	nahm	genommen	*take*
sprechen(i)	sprach	gesprochen	*speak*
stehlen(ie)	stahl	gestohlen	*steal*
*sterben(i)	starb	gestorben	*die*
treffen(i)	traf	getroffen	*hit, meet*
*werden(i)	wurde	geworden	*become*
werfen(i)	warf	geworfen	*throw*
*kommen	kam	gekommen	*come*
beginnen	begann	begonnen	*begin*
gewinnen	gewann	gewonnen	*win*
schwimmen	schwamm	geschwommen	*swim*

[1] The vowels in brackets in this and succeeding Groups after the infinitive represent second and third person singular of the present.
[2] Erschrecken *to frighten some one*, is a weak verb.
[3] ich nehme, du nimmst, er nimmt.

Group V

Infinitive	Imperfect	Past Part.	English
e	a	e	
essen(i)	aß	gegessen	*eat*
geben(i)	gab	gegeben	*give*
*geschehen(ie)	geschah	geschehen	*happen*
lesen(ie)	las	gelesen	*read*
messen(i)	maß	gemessen	*measure*
sehen (ie)	sah	gesehen	*see*
*treten(i)[1]	trat	getreten	*tread, step*
vergessen(i)	vergaß	vergessen	*forget*
bitten	bat	gebeten	*ask, beg*
sitzen	saß	gesessen	*sit*
besitzen	besaß	besessen	*possess, enjoy*
liegen	lag	gelegen	*lie*

[1] ich trete, du trittst, er tritt.

Group VI

Infinitive	Imperfect	Past Part.	English
a	u	a	
*fahren(ä)	fuhr	gefahren	*drive (fare)*
graben(ä)	grub	gegraben	*dig (grave)*
laden(ä)	lud	geladen	*load*
schaffen[1]	schuf	geschaffen	*create (shape)*
schlagen(ä)	schlug	geschlagen	*beat, strike (slay)*
tragen(ä)	trug	getragen	*carry, wear, bear*
*wachsen(ä)	wuchs	gewachsen	*grow*
waschen(ä)	wusch	gewaschen	*wash*

[1] **schaffen** *to get, work, manage* is a weak verb.

Group VII

Infinitive	Imperfect	Past Part.	English
a	ie, i	a	
*fallen(ä)	fiel	gefallen	*fall*
fangen(ä)	fing	gefangen	*catch, seize*
halten(ä)	hielt	gehalten	*hold, keep*
hangen(ä)[1]	hing	gehangen	*be hanging*
lassen(ä)	ließ	gelassen	*let, leave*
raten(ä)	riet	geraten	*advise, guess*
schlafen(ä)	schlief	geschlafen	*sleep*

[1] Note: **hängen, hängte, gehängt** *to hang* (trans.).

Group VIII

Infinitive	Imperfect	Past Part.	English
*laufen(äu)	lief	gelaufen	*run*
stoßen	stieß	gestoßen	*push*
rufen	rief	gerufen	*call*
*gehen	ging	gegangen	*go*
stehen	stand	gestanden	*stand*
tun	tat	getan	*do*

Irregular Weak Verbs

Infinitive	Imperfect	Past Part.	English
brennen	brannte	gebrannt	*burn*
kennen	kannte	gekannt	*know*
nennen	nannte	genannt	*call, tell*
*rennen	rannte	gerannt	*run*
senden	sandte	gesandt	*send*
wenden	wandte	gewandt	*turn*
bringen	brachte	gebracht	*bring*
denken	dachte	gedacht	*think*
können	konnte	gekonnt	*can, be able*
müssen	mußte	gemußt	*must, have to*
dürfen	durfte	gedurft	*may, be allowed*
wollen	wollte	gewollt	*want*
wissen	wußte	gewußt	*know*
sollen	sollte	gesollt	*ought to*
mögen	mochte	gemocht	*may, like*

ADVERBS

General rule: Most German adjectives are used as adverbs, and are then never inflected. The comparative of adverbs is the same as that of adjectives (-er), but the superlative must be preceded by **am** (for **an dem**) with the inflexion -en: **am schönsten** *most beautifully*.

Irregular comparison

bald *soon*	**eher** *sooner*	**am ehesten** *soonest*
viel *much*	**mehr** *more*	**am meisten** *most*
gut/wohl *well*	**besser** *better*	**am besten** *best*
gern *willingly*	**lieber** *rather*	**am liebsten** *best, most willingly*
wenig *little*	$\begin{cases}\textbf{weniger}\\\textbf{minder}\end{cases}$ *less*	$\begin{cases}\textbf{am wenigsten}\\\textbf{am mindesten}\end{cases}$ *least*

Also: **ehestens, höchstens, meistens, wenigstens** (translate: (*at*) *the earliest, highest, most, least*, etc.). And **meist** *mostly*.

The adverb never comes between the subject and the verb, as it often does in English.

Noch: *yet, still more*. Always precedes the word it qualifies.

> **Geben Sie mir noch Wasser.** *Give me some more water.*
> **Sind Sie noch hier?** *Are you still here?*

Much: translate by **viel** for quantity and **sehr** for intensity.

> **viel Wein** *much wine*   **sehr beliebt** *much loved*

Gern: used with a verb corresponds to English, *I like to.*

> **Ich spreche gern deutsch.** *I like to speak German.*
> **Ich spiele lieber.** *I prefer to play.*

PREPOSITIONS

The chief characteristic of German prepositions is that they govern cases—the genitive, dative, or accusative—in other words, their nouns must be put into the particular cases governed by the preposition.

PREPOSITIONS WITH THE GENITIVE

Er wohnt	**außerhalb** der Stadt. He lives *outside* the town.
Er wurde reich	**innerhalb** eines Jahres. He became rich *within* a year.
Er wohnt	**diesseits** der Mauer. He lives *on this side of* the Wall.
Sie wohnt	**jenseits** der Mauer.
	She lives *on the other side of* the Wall.
Er kommt	**(an)statt** seines Freundes.
	He is coming *instead of* his friend.
Sie kommen	**trotz** des Regens. They are coming *in spite of* the rain.
Er kommt nicht	**wegen** der Kälte. He is not coming *on account of* the cold.
Er arbeitet	**während** der Nacht. He works *during* the night.
Bäume stehen	**längs** der Straße. Trees stand *the length of* the street.

PREPOSITIONS WITH THE DATIVE

Er kommt	**aus** dem Hause. He is coming *out of* the house.
Ich kenne niemand	**außer** dir. I know no one *except* you.
Er wohnt	**bei** meinem Bruder. He lives *at* my brother's (house).
Der Post	**gegenüber** steht ein Hotel.
	Opposite the post office is a hotel.
Er kommt	**mit** seiner Freundin. He is coming *with* his girl-friend.
Wir gehen gleich	**nach** dem Essen.
	We are going directly *after* the meal.
Wir kennen uns	**seit** dem Krieg.
	We have known each other *since* the war.
Was wissen Sie	**von** diesem Mann? What do you know *about* this man?
Mein Sohn geht	**zur (zu der)** Schule. My son goes *to* school.
Note:	**zu Hause** *at home* **nach Hause** *home(wards)*
	zu Fuß *on foot* **zu Mittag** *at noon*

PREPOSITIONS WITH THE ACCUSATIVE

Er lief	**durch** die Stadt.	He ran *through* the town.
Dieses Buch ist	**für** Sie.	This book is *for* you.
Er fuhr seinen Auto	**gegen** einen Baum.	He drove his car *against* a tree.
Fritz kommt	**ohne** seine Mutter.	
		Fritz is coming *without* his mother
Wir sitzen	**um** den Tisch.	We are sitting *around* the table.
Er ist	**wider** diese Regel.	He is *against* this rule.

PREPOSITIONS WITH THE DATIVE
OR THE ACCUSATIVE

Motion (accus.)	Position (dat.)
Er geht **an** den Tisch.	Er sitzt **an** dem Tisch.
Er legt sein Buch **auf** den Stuhl.	Sein Buch liegt **auf** dem Stuhl.
Er geht **hinter** das Haus.	Er wartet **hinter** dem Haus.
Stellen Sie den Stuhl **neben** den Tisch!	Der Stuhl steht **neben** dem Tisch.
Sie geht **ins** (= in das) Büro.	Sie arbeitet **im** (= in dem) Büro.
Das Flugzeug fliegt **über** das Meer.	Das Flugzeug fliegt **über** dem Meer.
Die Katze springt **unter** das Bett.	Die Katze schläft **unter** dem Bett.
Fahren Sie den Wagen **vor** die Tür!	Ihr Wagen steht **vor** der Tür.
Stellen Sie die Lampe **zwischen** den Stuhl und das Sofa!	Die Lampe steht **zwischen** dem Stuhl und dem Sofa.

English:

He goes *to* the table.	He is sitting *at* the table.
He puts his book *on* to the table.	His book is (lying) *on* the table.
He goes *behind* the house.	He waits *behind* the house.
Put the chair *next to* the table.	The chair is *next to* the table.
She goes *into* the office.	She works *in* the office.
The plane is flying *across* the sea.	The plane is flying *above* the sea.
The cat leaps *under* the bed.	The cat is sleeping *under* the bed.
Drive the car *up to* the door.	Your car is *in front of* the door.
Put the lamp *between* the chair and the sofa.	The lamp is *between* the chair and the sofa.

CONJUNCTIONS

Conjunctions may conveniently be divided into two classes:
(i) Those which do not alter the construction of a sentence.
(ii) Those which alter it.

1. The following conjunctions do not affect construction and are called co-ordinating conjunctions:

Er versuchte es, **aber (allein)** er konnte es nicht.
He tried *but* he couldn't.

Er verkauft sein Auto, **denn** er braucht das Geld.
He is selling his car *because* he needs the money.

Wir gehen ins Kino **und** dann gehen wir schlafen.
We're going to the cinema *and* then we're going to bed.

Bleibst du hier **oder** gehst du mit?
Are you staying here *or* are you coming along?

Er gibt es mir nicht, **sondern** er leiht es mir nur.
He's not giving it to me *but* just lending it to me.

Also:

entweder ... oder ...	*either ... or ...*
weder ... noch ...	*neither ... nor ...*
sowohl ... als (auch)	*both ... and ...*

Aber or **sondern**?

Aber should always be used for *but*, except when there is a contrast to be expressed:

Sie ist nicht die Schwester **sondern** die Tochter.
She is not the sister *but* the daughter.

2. The following conjunctions send the verb to the end of the clause and are called subordinating conjunctions:

als *when, as*		**nachdem** *after*	
als ob *as if*		**ob** *whether*	
bevor⎫		**obwohl**⎫	
ehe ⎬ *before*		**obgleich**⎬ *although*	
bis *until*		**seit** ⎫	
da *as, since (a reason)*		**seitdem**⎬ *since*	
daß *that*		**während** *while*	
damit *so that*		**weil** *because*	
falls *in case*		**wenn** *when*	

indem *while*

Also all the question-words which become conjunctions in indirect speech:

wann *when*   **warum** *why*
was *what*   **wie** *how*
wo *where*

Es war 10 Uhr, **als** ich nach Hause **kam**. *It was 10 o'clock when I came home.*
Sie sagt, **daß** sie nicht kommen **kann**. *She says that she can't come.*
Ich weiß nicht, **was** er morgen **macht**. *I don't know what he's doing tomorrow.*
Sie weiß nicht, **warum** er nicht **kommt**. *She doesn't know why he's not coming.*

Wann, wenn or als?
Wann is used in direct or indirect questions:

Wann kommt er? Ich weiß nicht, wann er kommt. *When is he coming? I don't know when he's coming.*

Wenn is used to express *whenever* or *if*:

Ich werde es ihm sagen, wenn ich ihn sehe. *I'll tell him if I see him.*
Er war immer mit ihr, wenn ich ihn sah. *He was always with her when(ever) I saw him.*

Als refers to a definite past occasion:

Als ich den Brief schrieb, war ich sehr müde. *When I wrote the letter I was very tired.*

IDIOMS

A few common idioms are given below as examples, and others will be found in Part II (page 68). Many idioms will also be found in the Vocabulary (pages 71–107), under their respective words.

Sie haben recht (unrecht).	*You are right (wrong).*
Mir ist heiß (kalt).	*I am hot (cold).*
Ich habe Durst (Hunger).	*I am thirsty (hungry).*
Bitte (in reply to, '*Excuse me.*'	*Don't mention it.*
'*Pardon me.*')	
Wir haben es eilig.	*We are in a hurry*
Was heißt das?	*What does that mean?*
Was ist los?	*What's the matter?*
Beeilen Sie sich!	*Hurry up.*
Ich bedaure sehr.	*I'm very sorry.*
Ich glaube ja.	*I believe so.*
Es paßte uns sehr gut.	*It suited us very well.*
Was haben Sie?	*What is the matter with you?*
Danke sehr.	*Thank you very much.*
Wie sagt man das auf deutsch?	*How do you say that in German?*

CORRESPONDENCE

The date is written thus: **den 3. Juni 1966, den 25. Dez. 1967** *the 3rd June 1966, 25th Dec. 1967.*
A formal opening: **Sehr geehrter Herr!** *Dear Sir.*
A moderately familiar opening: **Sehr geehrter Herr Schmidt!**
Sehr geehrte gnädige Frau! *Dear Madam*, etc.
A familiar opening: **Mein lieber X!**
A business-like ending: **Hochachtungsvoll.**
A formal one: **Mit vorzüglicher Hochachtung.**
A moderately familiar ending: **Ihr ergebener ... or Ihr ...**
With best wishes: **Mit bestem Gruß.**
With kind regards: **Mit freundlichen Grüßen.**
Address envelopes thus:

> Herrn (Frau, Fräulein)
>   A. Müller,
> 1 <u>BERLIN</u> 30,
>   Prinzregentenstraße 40.

WORD-BUILDING*

CAPACITY OF GERMAN FOR WORD-BUILDING

Its truly remarkable capacity for forming derivative and compound words is one of the chief characteristics of German. From the point of view of the foreign learner it is at the same time a difficulty and an encouragement: a difficulty because of the large number of irregularities which can only be mastered by long experience; and an encouragement because of the wide vocabulary which rapidly comes within the bounds of comprehension.

When the 'Basis of Grammar' and the 'Essential' or 'root' vocabulary are known, and the principles of word-formation outlined below mastered, the meaning of thousands of words can be conjectured with fair certainty, and of many other thousands with absolute confidence.

Take the compound word

Lebensversicherungsgesellschaft.

Such a word may at first appear somewhat terrifying. It need not be so. The first thing to appreciate about all such long words is that the compound exists only for the *eye*: when spoken it is divided into *groups*; and, in actual conversation, it is as easy to utter as its English equivalent 'Life Insurance Company'. Nor is it very dissimilar when we come to analyse it:

Lebens-	This is the genitive case of **das Leben** *life*.
-ver-	An inseparable prefix (see page 60) meaning *intensification*.
-sicher-	An adjective meaning *sure*.
-ungs-	A suffix (see page 61) corresponding to English *-ing*.
-gesell-	A noun meaning *companion, associate member*. (ge- is an inseparable prefix denoting a *union* or putting together.) (See page 60.)
-schaft	A suffix corresponding to the English ending *-ship* in such words as *friendship*, etc. (See page 61.)

---

* Some German words given under 'Word-building' as examples are not included in the Vocabulary on pages 71–107, not being 'essential'.

Clearly these words and particles strung together could hardly have any other meaning but 'Life Insurance Company'. And so,

Hamburg-Südamerikanische Dampfschiffahrtsgesellschaft

for 'Hamburg-South America Steamship Company'.

THE FOUR WAYS OF WORD-BUILDING

There are, for practical purposes, four ways of making new words by deriving and compounding:

1. By changing the root vowel: **die Fähre** *the ferry*, from **fahren** *to go, drive*.

2. By adding a suffix or ending: **kostbar** *costly*, *precious*, from **kosten** *to cost* and the ending -bar. **Kostbarkeit** *costliness*.

3. By a prefix: **das Einkommen** *income*, from **kommen** *to come*, with the prefix **ein-**, exactly as in English.

4. By putting together two or more quite independent words: **das Nebelhorn** *the fog-horn*.

One can see that these principles exist in English:

die Höhe *height*	from **hoch** *high*
die Güte *goodness*	from **gut** *good*
der Biß *the bite*	from **beißen** *to bite*
das Schicksal *fate*	from **schicken** *to send*
die Finsternis *darkness*	from **finster** *dark* and **-nis** *-ness*

The list of examples could be extended indefinitely. The student should now glance at the sample group of words springing from **kommen** on page 62.

It will be noticed that nouns can be formed from adjectives, verbs, etc., and vice versa: and that there is, indeed, great liberty in the formation of one part of speech from another, or in compounding.

PREFIXES USED IN WORD-BUILDING

All the inseparable prefixes are employed: **be-, ent-, emp-, er- (ur-), ge-, miß-, ver-,** and **zer-.** It is not possible here to cover all the shades of meaning which these prefixes denote, but the following examples give some idea of their scope:

be- (English *be-*) to give or apply to, to provide with, to complete: **bekleiden** *to clothe*, **beraten** *to 'ply' with advice, to counsel*, **belachen** *to laugh at*, **bedecken** *to deck out, cover with*.

ent- removal or depriving, also denotes transition or a change of state:
(emp-) **enthaupten** *to behead*, **entschuldigen** *to remove blame* (**Schuld**) *from*, **entflammen** *to burst into flame*.

er- out, out from, completion of a process, also original or primeval:
(ur-) **erdenken** *to think out, evolve*, **erfinden** *to find out, invent*, **Urmensch** *primeval man*, **Urwald** *primeval forest*, **uralt** *extremely ancient*, **erfüllen** *to fulfil*, **erhören** *to give a hearing to*, **erkranken** *to fall ill*, **erbleichen** *to grow pale*.

ge- A collective: **gerinnen** *to run together, to curdle*, **Gefolge** *the following, attendance*.

miß- (English *mis-*) denotes failure, something wrong, and often, a perversion: **mißbrauchen** *to misuse*, **Mißbildung** *deformity*, **Mißerfolg** *failure*.

ver- (English *for-*) away, negative, and also an intensification of an existing state: **blühen** *to bloom*, **verblühen** *to fade*, **bieten** *to bid, offer*, **verbieten** *to forbid*, **lernen** *to learn*, **verlernen** *to unlearn, forget*, **veralten** *to become antiquated, grow old*, **menschlich** *human*, **vermenschlichen** *to humanize*.

wider- (English *with-*) against: **widerstehen** *to withstand*, **widersprechen** *to contradict*.

zer- asunder, with some violence: **zergliedern** *to dismember*, **zerreißen** *to tear to pieces*, **zertreten** *to crush*.

In the same way many thousands of words are made with the separable prefixes given on page 44. **Aufstehen** *to get up*, **herkommen** *to come hither*, **zusammenkommen** *to come together*. And so forth. The meaning of words made with these separable prefixes is much more easily recognized than of those made with the inseparable—because the meanings of the separable prefixes are more fixed and less vague.

SUFFIXES USED IN WORD-BUILDING

A number of suffixes are added to 'root' words to make other words. Of these the following are the most important.

Suffix	Gender	Meanings	Examples
ei-	F	(a) a slur	**Kinderei** *childishness*
		(b) place	**Buchbinderei** *book-bindery, book-binding*
		(c) product or craft	**Bäckerei** *bakery, baker's craft*

-chen⎱ -lein⎰	N	diminutives	⎰Kindlein *little child* ⎱Männchen *manikin*
-ling	M	-ling	Findling *foundling*
-nis	F or N	-ness	Finsternis *darkness*
-in	F	-ess	Göttin *goddess*
-ung	F	-ing	Schulung *schooling*
-er	M	-er	Berliner *Berliner*
*-heit⎱ *-keit⎰	F	⎰-hood, head ⎱-ness, etc.	Kindheit *childhood* Dankbarkeit *thankfulness*
*-schaft	F	-ship, etc.	Freundschaft *friendship*
*-tum	M or N	-dom	Königtum *kingdom*

* Form abstract nouns.

Note the adjectival endings:

-lich	-ly, -like	täglich *daily*
-ig	-y	blutig *bloody*
-isch	-ish	kindisch *childish*
-bar	-able, -ible, -ful	eßbar *edible*

It should be clearly understood that the above statement contains merely the basic and essential principles of the German system of word-building, and not an exhaustive treatment, for which a treatise would be required. What is given is intended chiefly as a *demonstration* of the extremely convenient and flexible methods used in the making of vocabulary. But, with what has been given, and the 'Essential Vocabulary' in the following pages, the student has a very remarkable instrument at his disposal for reading purposes. To guess at the meaning of a word is often to court disaster. Yet the percentage of words of which the meaning can be correctly worked out when the above principles are known, is considerable. Always go for the 'root' or 'roots' of a compound word. Then take it to pieces, and it will generally become clear.

An example of an essential word and its 'group'

To illustrate further the very important principles stated, some of the derivatives and compounds of the 'essential' verb **kommen** are give below. Again, this is not an exhaustive statement, merely an illustrative one.

kommen *to come;* **kam; gekommen.**

Nouns:	das Einkommen	*income*
	der Nachkomme	*descendant*
	das Unterkommen	*shelter*
	die Nachkommenschaft	*offspring, issue*
	das Vorkommnis	*event, occurrence*
	die Zuvorkommenheit	*politeness*
	das Willkommen	*welcome*
	die Abkunft	*origin, descent*
	die Übereinkunft	*agreement*
	die Zukunft	*future*
	der Zukünftige	*future husband, fiancé*
	die Ankunft	*arrival*
	das Herkommen	*tradition*
	die Herkunft	*origin*
	die Auskunft	*information*
Verbs:	ankommen	*arrive*
	bekommen	*come by, obtain*
	entkommen	*escape*
	entgegenkommen	*meet, treat kindly*
	übereinkommen	*agree*
	unterkommen	*find shelter, obtain a position*
	verkommen	*to go to the bad, to the dogs*
	zuvorkommen	*be beforehand, prevent*
Adjec-	willkommen	*welcome*
tives and	abkömmlich	*dispensable*
adverbs:	herkömmlich	*traditional*
	zukünftig	*future*

LEARNING A VOCABULARY

On the model of **kommen** the student is advised to make up his own groups of words as he progresses in the language. Keep a notebook and enter new words under the 'root' or basic word. (See Part II, page 70 for further hints.) Look up in the Vocabulary (pages 71–107): **das Land** *land*, **die Hand** *hand*, **die Heimat** *(native) home*, and any other root-words you may fancy. Make 'group-lists' and go over them until you know them.

SENTENCE

The student is advised to be content at first to form only sentences of a simple, straightforward nature, and to avoid grammatical subtleties. Six rules, all of them of vital importance, must in the end be learnt:

1. Infinitives and past participles in compound tenses are placed at the *end*. When there is both an infinitive and past participle, the infinitive stands last.

> **Ich habe einen Apfel gegessen.** *I have eaten an apple.*
> **Ich werde den Apfel gegessen haben.** *I shall have eaten the apple.*

2. Dative noun precedes accusative, but accusative pronoun precedes dative.

> **Der Vater hat dem Kinde ein Buch gegeben.** *The father has given the child a book.*
> **Er gab es ihm.** *He gave it to him.*

3. A pronoun object precedes a noun object.

> **Der Vater gab ihm ein Buch.** *The father gave him a book.*

4. Adverbs of time follow a simple tense or an auxiliary, but pronouns *precede* them.

> **Der Vater hat gestern dem Kind ein Buch gegeben.** *The father gave a book to the child yesterday.*
> **Der Vater gab ihm gestern ein Buch.** *The father gave him a book yesterday.*

5. Adverbs are placed in order of *time, manner, place*.

> **Er kam gestern müde nach Hause.** *He came home tired yesterday.*

6. **Nicht** precedes the word it negatives, but follows an accusative, an adverb of *time*, or a simple verb.

> **Das Kind kann nicht alles machen.** *The child cannot do everything.*
> **Das Kind sah den Vater nicht.** *The child did not see the father.*
> **Ich habe das Kind lange nicht gesehen.** *I have not seen the child for a long time.*
> **Ich weiß nicht.** *I do not know.*

Inversion

For emphasis or variety of style, a word which is not the subject may be placed first in a sentence, and then the subject is placed *after* the simple verb or auxiliary. For the remainder of the sentence the rules already stated apply.

> **Zu Weihnachten gab der Vater dem Kinde ein Buch.** *It was at Christmas that the father gave the child a book.*

Note: See page 30 for sentences following a relative pronoun, and pages 54–5 for sentences introduced by conjunctions.

*   *   *

The best way to avoid having to make complex sentences in German is to simplify the thought down to bare essentials. Thus, 'Even though John was ill, he still came to see us,' can be rendered: 'John was ill but he came to see us.'

PART II

THE ESSENTIAL VOCABULARY

ESSENTIAL VOCABULARY

The main body of Essential Vocabulary is given on pages 71–107.

But note that certain words which recur very frequently are omitted from the main body of Vocabulary: these have already been given in Part I, and it is assumed that they have been memorized. Also omitted are certain other words. These are listed below. A summary of omissions from the main Vocabulary is given here for convenience.

1. The comparative and superlative forms of adjectives, given on page 23.
2. The numeral words given on pages 25–6.
3. The pronouns given on pages 27–33.
4. Some little-used compound words given as illustration of Word Building on pages 58–62.
5. A limited number of words for names of countries, geographical adjectives, and nouns of nationality, etc. A list of these is given below for reference.
6. Days of the week, months of the year, and seasons—given below for memorizing.

All of these omissions from the main body of the Vocabulary are important (except the fourth category), and the words included in them must be known.

Greetings and some everyday locutions are also listed below.

List of nationalities and geographical words

Afrika *Africa*	**afrikanisch** *African*	**Afrikaner** (-)
Amerika *America*	**amerikanisch** *American*	**Amerikaner** (-)
Asien *Asia*	**asiatisch** *Asiatic*	**Asiate** (-n) (w.n.)
Australien *Australia*	**australisch** *Australian*	**Australier** (-)
Europa *Europe*	**europäisch** *European*	**Europäer** (-)
Belgien *Belgium*	**belgisch** *Belgian*	**Belgier** (-)
China *China*	**chinesisch** *Chinese*	**Chinese** (-n) (w.n.)
Deutschland *Germany*	**deutsch** *German*	**Deutscher** (a.n.)
England *England*	**englisch** *English*	**Engländer** (-)
Frankreich *France*	**französisch** *French*	**Franzose** (-n)
Großbritannien *Great Britain*	**britisch** *British*	**Brite** (-n) (w.n.)
Holland *Holland*	**holländisch** *Dutch*	**Holländer** (-)
Irland *Ireland*	**irisch** *Irish*	**Ire** (-) (w.n.) or **Irländer** (-)

Italien *Italy*	italienisch *Italian*	Italiener (-)
Jugoslavien *Jugoslavia*	jugoslawisch *Jugoslavian*	Jugoslawe (-n) (w.n.)
Norwegen *Norway*	norwegisch *Norwegian*	Norweger (-)
Österreich *Austria*	österreichisch *Austrian*	Österreicher (-)
Polen *Poland*	polnisch *Polish*	Pole (-n) (w.n.)
Rußland *Russia*	russisch *Russian*	Russe (-n) (w.n.)
Schottland *Scotland*	schottisch *Scottish*	Schotte (-n) (w.n.)
Schweden *Sweden*	schwedisch *Swedish*	Schwede (-n) (w.n.)
die Schweiz *Switzerland*	schweizerisch *Swiss*	Schweizer (-)
Spanien *Spain*	spanisch *Spanish*	Spanier (-)
Ungarn *Hungary*	ungarisch *Hungarian*	Ungar (-n) (w.n.)

die Sowjetunion *Soviet Union* der Nahe Osten *Near East*
die Vereinigten Staaten *United States* der Ferne Osten *Far East*
die Deutsche Demokratische die Bundesrepublik Deutschland
  Republik (DDR) *German*   *German Federal Republic*
  Democratic Republic

Aachen *Aix-le-Chapelle*	Moskau *Moscow*
Antwerpen *Antwerp*	München *Munich*
Basel *Basle, Bale*	Nürnberg *Nuremberg*
Brüssel *Brussels*	Venedig *Venice*
Den Haag *The Hague*	Warschau *Warsaw*
Köln *Cologne*	Wien *Vienna*
Lüttich *Liége*	

Days of the week, months, and seasons

der Sonntag *Sunday*. Montag *Monday*. Dienstag *Tuesday*. Mittwoch *Wednesday*. Donnerstag *Thursday*. Freitag *Friday*. Samstag *Saturday, in South Germany, Austria and the Rhineland*. Sonnabend *Saturday, elsewhere in Germany and in Switzerland*.

Januar (Jänner *in Austria*). Februar. März. April. Mai. Juni. Juli. August. September. Oktober. November. Dezember.

der Frühling *spring* der Herbst *autumn*
der Sommer *summer* der Winter *winter*

Greetings and everyday locutions

Guten Morgen *Good morning* Haben Sie die Güte . . . *Be so kind as . . .*
Guten Tag *Good day, good afternoon* Herr (*name*) *Mr.*
Guten Abend *Good evening* Frau (*name*) *Mrs.*
Gute Nacht *Good night* Fräulein (*name*) *Miss*
Wie geht es Ihnen? or Wie geht es? Ach! *Ah! Oh!*
  How are you?   Ach so! *Is that so?* Or when rather
Gut. Sehr gut. *Well. Very well.*   taken aback on hearing sth.
Danke *Thanks, thank you.* Ach wo! *Certainly not. Impossible!*
Danke sehr, schön *Thank you very much.* Ja *yes* Jawohl *yes, indeed*

Bitte *Please* or *yes, please*
Also used for '*Don't mention it*' in reply to thanks; for '*I beg your pardon*' meaning '*What did you say?*', for '*Please do*', '*Please go ahead*', etc.
So! *Indeed? Really?*
Entschuldigen Sie *Excuse me.*
Verzeihen Sie *Pardon me.*
Auf Wiedersehen *Goodbye.*

Nein *no*
Doch *yes*, after negative or for emphasis
Ausgezeichnet! *Excellent*
Wirklich? *Really?*
Noch einmal *once more, once again*
Natürlich *Of course. Naturally.*
Darf ich Ihnen Herrn X vorstellen? *May I introduce Mr. X?*
Mit Vergnügen *With pleasure*
Achtung! *Attention! Take care!*
Passen Sie auf! *Look out!*
Na! *Well! Come now!*

Acquiring a German vocabulary

The *best* way to acquire a working vocabulary in any foreign language—and how to use it to best effect—is either by living where it is spoken all around one, or by constant practice with the help of a good speaker of that language. One must *hear the language spoken*, mimic the sounds heard, and have mispronunciations corrected. When such facilities are not available, there is no need to despair, but learning will be slower and more effort will be required. Once the pronunciation is known (pages 3–7), the beginner quickly realizes that many German words are similar to their English equivalents, which makes things easier. For example:

Nouns	Adjectives	Other words
der Ball *ball*	**braun** *brown*	**dann** *then*
der Berg *hill, mount*	**breit** *broad*	**für** *for*
berg (*in iceberg*)	**dünn** *thin*	**bevor** *before*
die Butter *butter*	**falsch** *false*	**hören** *to hear*
das Wasser *water*	**frei** *free*	**kosten** *to cost*

As you see, there are often slight differences, but you will find that they usually follow easily distinguishable patterns. Here is one constantly recurring set of patterns:

	1		2	3	4		5	6	
German:	z	ss ß	d	t	pf	f	b	k	ch
become	↓		↓	↓	↓		↓	↓	
English:	t		th	d	p		f v	k	

Examples:	1. zehn	Wasser	2. der	3. Tür	4. Pfund	reif
	ten	water	the	door	pound	ripe
	5. Leben	leben	6. König	wachen		
	life	to live	King	to wake		

This very brief statement indicates the most regular and most constant changes in consonants from German to English, and incidentally demonstrates the close relationship between the two languages. The learner of German quickly begins to realise that a large number of German words are so close to their English equivalents that they can be memorized almost without effort.

In regard to the memorizing of words in general, two more hints can be given:

1. When memorizing nouns (except abstract nouns) and verbs (excepting those relating to abstract concepts) is is usually possible to form an idea in the mind, a 'mind-picture', of the idea represented by the German word that is being learnt. Thus, when memorizing by saying aloud **das Meer** *the sea*, imagine yourself bathing in it on a pleasant summer's day, or diving into it, or engaged in a swimming-race: **das Meer** *the sea* will thus be planted in the memory. Similarly **tragen** *to carry*, also *to wear*, can be helped into the memory by imagining yourself carrying home a suit that you will soon be wearing. In this way, memorizing can be made easier.

2. Know all the words both ways: **die Zukunft**=*future*, and *the future*=**die Zukunft**. Say all German words aloud when learning them.

Essential strong and irregular verbs (pages 46–50): Learn these by groups, memorizing not more than ten verbs at a time. Most of these verbs are of very frequent occurrence.

ESSENTIAL VOCABULARY

German/English

For omissions from this Vocabulary, see page 67.
An article is given with all German nouns. The plural forms of nouns are indicated: **der Anfang** (*÷e*) *beginning*. A weak noun is indicated: **der Junge** (-n) (w.n.) **boy**. An adjectival noun: **der Mitreisende** (a.n.) *travelling companion*. Strong or irregular verbs are marked in accordance with the classification on pages 46–50, thus: **brechen** (iv) *to break*. Compound verbs follow the conjugation of their root verbs. A separable prefix is indicated by a hyphen: **ab-fliegen** *to take off*.

A

der Abend (-e) *evening*
aber *but*
die Abfahrt (-en) *departure*
ab-fliegen (ii) *to take off* (*plane*)
der Abort (-e) *lavatory, W.C., toilet*
ab-reisen *to leave* (*on journey*)
die Absicht (-en) *intention*
die Abteilung (-en) *section; department*
Acht geben *to pay attention*
die Achtung (-en) *attention; care*
Achtung! *Attention! Look out!*
ähnlich *similar*
der Akt (-e) *act* (*of a play*)
all (-e) (adj.) *all, every*, (*all gone, no more*)
alle beide *both*
Das Geld ist alle *The money's gone*
allein *alone*
allerdings *of course, surely*
allerlei *all kinds of*
allgemein *general*
6—B.E.G.

als *when, as, than*
als ob *as if* (see p. 54)
also *thus, therefore, so*
alt *old*
das Alter (-) *age, old age*
das Amt (*÷er*) *office, official position*
an (+ acc/dat) *at, on, to*
der Anblick (-e) *view, sight*
ändern *to change, alter*
anders *different, otherwise*
anderthalb *one and a half*
der Anfang (*÷e*) *beginning*
an-fangen (vii) *to begin*
angenehm *pleasant*
an-greifen (i) *to attack*
der Angriff (-e) *attack, aggression*
die Angst (*÷e*) *anxiety, fear*
an-halten (vii) *to stop*
an-klagen *to accuse*
an-kommen (iv) *to arrive*
die Ankunft (*÷e*) *arrival*
der Anlaß (Anlässe) *occasion*
an-nehmen (iv) *to accept, receive, adopt*

der Anruf (-e) *phone call*
an-rufen (viii) *to telephone*
an-sagen *to announce*
der Ansager (-) *announcer (radio etc.)*
an-schauen *to look at*
der Anschluß (Anschlüsse) *junction, union, connection*
an-sehen (v) *to look at*
die Ansicht (-en) *view, opinion*
der Anspruch (⸚e) *title, claim*
die Anstalt (-en) *institution*
anstatt (+ gen) *instead of*
die Antwort (-en) *answer*
antworten *to answer*
der Anwalt (⸚e) *lawyer, solicitor*
anwesend *present*
die Anzahl (-en) *number, quantity*
an-ziehen (ii) *to put on (clothes), to attract*
sich an-ziehen (ii) *to dress oneself*
der Anzug (⸚e) *suit, costume*
an-zünden *to light*
der Apfel (⸚) *apple*
die Apotheke (-n) *chemist's shop, pharmacy*
der Apotheker (-) *chemist, pharmacist*
der Apparat (-e) *apparatus (radio, T.V. set, telephone, etc.)*
die Arbeit (-en) *work*
der Arbeiter (-) *workman, worker*
arbeiten *to work*
der Arm (-e) *arm*
arm *poor*
die Armbanduhr (-en) *wrist watch*
die Armee (-n) *army*
die Armut *poverty*
die Art (-en) *kind, species, manner*
artig *well behaved, good*
der Artikel (-) *article*
der Arzt (⸚e) *physician, doctor*
die Asche (-n) *ashes, embers*
der Aschenbecher (-) *ashtray*
das Aspirin (-) *aspirin*

der Ast (⸚e) *branch*
der Atem *breath*
atmen *to breathe*
das Atom (-e) *atom*
auch *also*
auf (+ acc/dat) *upon*
auf sein *to be open*
auf-fallen (vii) *to strike, astonish*
auf-fassen *to grasp, understand*
der Aufenthalt (-e) *stay, sojourn*
die Aufgabe (-en) *task, exercise, assignment*
sich auf-halten (vii) *to stay*
auf-hören *to cease, stop*
auf-machen *to open*
aufmerksam *attentive*
die Aufmerksamkeit *attention*
aufrecht *erect, upright, straight*
auf-regen *to excite, stir up*
aufrichtig *sincere, honest*
auf-stehen (viii) *to get up, stand up, rise*
der Auftrag (⸚e) *order, errand*
der Aufzug (⸚e) *lift, elevator*
das Auge (-n) *eye*
der Augenblick (-e) *moment*
aus (+ dat) *out (of), from*
der Ausdruck (⸚e) *expression, word, phrase*
aus-drücken *to express*
der Ausflug (⸚e) *picnic, outing*
aus-führen *to carry out, complete*
der Ausgang (⸚e) *exit*
aus-gehen (viii) *to go out (for a walk)*
ausgezeichnet *excellent, fine*
die Auskunft (⸚e) *news, information*
das Ausland *foreign country*
im Ausland *abroad*
ins Ausland *abroad*
auslöschen *to put out, extinguish*
die Ausnahme (n) *exception*
die Aussprache (-n) *pronunciation*

aus-sprechen (iv) *to pronounce*
außen (adv) *outside, out of doors*
außer (+ dat) *except, without*
die Ausstellung (-en) *exhibition*
die Auswahl (-en) *choice, selection*
aus-wählen *to choose*
das Auto (-s) *motor car*
die Autobahn (-en) *motor-way*
der Autobus (-se) *motor bus*
der Autofahrer (-) *(car) driver*

B

der Bach (⁓e) *brook*
backen, backte, gebacken *to bake*
das Bad (⁓er) *bath, spa*
baden *to bathe*
die Bahn (-en) *road, path, way*
der Bahnhof (⁓e) *railway station*
der Bahnsteig (-e) *(railway) platform*
der Bahnübergang (⁓e) *level crossing*
bald *soon*
der Ball (⁓e) *dance, ball*
die Bank (-en) *bank (for money)*
die Bank (⁓e) *seat, bench*
die Bar (-s) *bar (drinking)*
bauen *to build*
der Bau (-ten) *building*
der Bauer (-n) (w.n.) *farmer, peasant*
die Bäuerin (-nen) *farmer's wife, peasant woman*
der Baum (⁓e) *tree*
die Baumwolle *cotton*
die Baustelle (-n) *building site*
der Beamte (a.n.) *official, civil servant*
der Becher (-) *tumbler, cup, beaker*
der Bedarf *need, requirement*
bedauern *to regret, pity*

bedecken *to cover*
bedeuten *to mean*
die Bedeutung (-en) *meaning, importance*
bedienen *to serve*
sich bedienen *to help oneself*
die Bedienung *service*
die Bedingung (-en) *condition, stipulation*
bedürfen (+ gen) *to need, require*
der Befehl (-e) *order, command*
befehlen (iv) (+ dat) *to order, command*
sich befinden *to be, feel (of health)*
befreien *to release, liberate*
befriedigen *to satisfy*
begegnen (+ dat) *to meet*
beginnen (iv) *to begin*
begleiten *to accompany*
begreifen (i) *to grasp (an idea)*
der Begriff (-e) *idea, conception*
behalten (vii) *to keep, retain*
bei (+ dat) *at, near, with, beside*
beide *both, the two*
das Bein (-e) *bone, leg*
beißen (i) *to bite*
das Beispiel (-e) *example*
zum Beispiel *for example*
bekannt (adj.) *known, famous*
der/die Bekannte (a.n.) *acquaintance*
die Bekanntschaft *circle (of acquaintances)*
sich beklagen *to complain*
bekommen (iv) *to get, receive, obtain*
beliebt *popular*
bemerken *to catch sight of, notice, remark*
die Bemerkung (-en) *remark*
bemühen *to trouble*
sich bemühen *to try hard*
das Benzin *petrol, gasoline*
beobachten *to watch, observe*
bequem *comfortable*
bereit *ready, prepared*

bereiten *to prepare*
bereits *already*
der Berg (-e) *mountain*
bergab *downhill*
bergauf *uphill*
der Bericht (-e) *report*
berichten *to report*
der Beruf (-e) *occupation, profession*
berühmt *famous, celebrated*
beschäftig *busy*
beschließen (ii) *to decide*
beschreiben (i) *to describe*
besetzt *occupied*
der Besitz (-e) *possession, wealth, property*
besitzen (v) *to possess, own*
besonder(s) *special(ly)*
besser, beste, *better, best*
bestehen auf (+ acc) (viii) *to insist on*
bestehen aus (+ dat) (viii) *to consist of*
bestellen *to order, engage*
bestimmen *to decide, fix*
bestimmt *definite, intended*
der Besuch (-e) *visit*
besuchen *to visit*
beten *to pray*
der Betrag (ᵉe) *sum, amount*
der Betrieb (-e) *firm, factory*
sich betrinken (iii) *to get drunk*
das Bett (-en) *bed*
zu Bett gehen *to go to bed*
bevor *before* (see p. 54)
bewegen *to move, stir*
die Bewegung (-en) *movement, motion*
der Beweis (-e) *proof*
beweisen (i) *to prove*
bewohnen *to inhabit*
der Bewohner (-) *inhabitant*
bewundern *to admire*
bewußt *aware, conscious*
bezahlen *to pay*

die Beziehung *connection*
in Beziehung auf *in relation to, with regard to*
der Bezirk (-e) *district*
die Bibliothek (-en) *library*
biegen (i) *to bend*
das Bier (-e) *beer*
bieten (ii) *to offer, bid*
das Bild (-er) *picture*
bilden *to form, educate*
die Bildung (-en) *education, culture*
billig *cheap*
binden (iii) *to bind, tie*
die Birne (-n) (1) *pear*, (2) *electric bulb*
bis *till, until* (see p. 54)
bisher *till now*
ein bißchen *a little, bit, morsel*
die Bitte (-n) *request*
bitte *please*
bitten (v) *to ask (a favour), to request*
blaß *pale*
das Blatt (ᵉer) (1) *leaf;* (2) *sheet of paper*
blau *blue*
das Blei *lead*
bleiben (i) *to remain*
bleich *pale*
der Bleistift (-e) *(lead) pencil*
der Blick (-e) *look, glance*
blicken *to look at, glance at*
blind *blind*
der Blitz (-e) *flash, lightning*
blitzen *to flash, lighten*
blond *fair, blond(e)*
bloß *merely, only, bare, naked*
blühen *to bloom*
die Blume (-n) *flower*
die Bluse (-n) *blouse*
das Blut *blood*
der Boden (ᵉ) *floor, ground*
das Boot (-e) *boat*
böse *evil, wicked*
böse auf (+ acc) *angry with*

der **Bote** (-n) (w.n.) *messenger*
die **Botschaft** (-en) *embassy, message*
das **Boxen** *boxing*
boxen *to box*
braten *to roast*
die **Bratkartoffel** (-n) *roast potato*
brauchen *to need, require*
braun *brown*
die **Braut** (ˉe) *fiancée, bride*
der **Bräutigam** (-e) *fiancé, bridegroom*
brechen (iv) *to break*
breit *broad, wide*
die **Bremse** (-n) *brake*
brennen (irr. p. 50) *to burn*
der **Brief** (-e) *letter*
der **Briefkasten** (-) *letterbox*
die **Briefmarke** (-n) *postage stamp*
der **Briefträger** (-) *postman*
der **Briefwechsel** *correspondence*
die **Brille** (-n) (*pair of*) *spectacles, glasses*
bringen (irr. p. 50) *to bring, carry*
das **Brot** (-e) *bread*
die **Brücke** (-n) *bridge*
der **Bruder** (ˉ) *brother*
der **Brunnen** (-) *well, fountain*
die **Brust** (ˉe) *breast, chest*
das **Buch** (ˉer) *book*
der **Buchhändler** (-) *bookseller*
die **Buchhandlung** (-en) *bookshop*
bügeln *to iron*
der **Bund** (ˉe) *alliance, league, federation*
die **Bundesrepublik** *Federal Republic (W. Germany)*
bunt *coloured, colourful*
die **Burg** (-en) *castle*
der **Bürger** (-) *citizen*
der **Bürgermeister** (-) *mayor*
das **Büro** (-s) *office*
der **Bursche** (-n) (w.n.) *fellow, chap*
die **Bürste** (-n) *brush*

der **Busch** (ˉe) *bush, shrub*
die **Butter** *butter*
das **Butterbrot** (-e) *bread and butter, sandwich*

C

das **Café** (-s) *café*
der **Charakter** (-e) *character, disposition*
der **Chauffeur** (-e) *chauffeur, driver*
der **Chef** (-s) *chief, head (of firm), boss*
die **Chemie** *chemistry*

D

da (adv) *there* (conj) *as, when, because, since* see p. 54)
da- (adv + preps makes many compounds such as:—**dabei** *there, at it, at that*)
das **Dach** (ˉer) *roof*
dadurch *through it, thereby*
dafür *for that, for it*
dagegen *against it*
daher *therefore, along*
dahin *there, thither*
damals *at that time, then*
die **Dame** (-n) *lady*
damit *with it, in order that* (see p. 54)
dämmern *to grow dark, to dawn*
die **Dämmerung** (-en) *twilight, dusk*
der **Dampf** (ˉe) *vapour, steam*
der **Dampfer** (-) *steamer (ship)*
der **Dank** *thanks*
dankbar *thankful*
danken (+ dat) *to thank*
dann *then, after that*
daran *at it, at them*

darauf *on it, them, thereupon*
daraus *out of it, them*
darin *in it, them*
darüber *over it, them*
darum *therefore*
darunter *under it, them*
daß *that* (see p. 54)
das **Datum** *date,* pl. **Daten** *facts, data*
dauern *to last, continue*
davon *from it, them*
davor *in front of it, them*
dazu *to it, them*
dazwischen *between it, them*
die **Decke** (-n) *blanket, cover, ceiling*
decken *to cover*
demokratisch *democratic*
denken (irr. p. 50) *to think*
denn *for, because, as (since)*
derselbe (die-, das-, pl. dieselben) *the same*
deshalb *therefore*
desto *so much.* See **je ...**
deswegen *therefore*
deutlich *distinct(ly), clear(ly)*
deutsch *German*
dicht *close, dense, tight, compact*
der **Dichter** (-) *poet, author*
dick *thick, stout, fat*
der **Dieb** (-e) *thief*
dienen (+dat) *to serve*
der **Dienst** (-e) *service*
dies- *this* (see p. 11)
diesseits (+gen) *(on) this side of*
das **Ding** (-e) *thing, gadget*
direkt *direct*
der **Direktor** (-en) *manager, director*
doch (1) *but, yet* (intensifying), (2) *yes* (contradicting a negative); (3) *however*
der **Dollar** (-s) *dollar* ($)

der **Dolmetscher** (-) *interpreter*
dolmetschen *to interpret*
der **Dom** (-e) *cathedral*
der **Donner** (-) *thunder*
donnern *to thunder*
doppelt *double*
das **Dorf** (⸚er) *village*
der **Dorn** (-e/-er) *thorn*
dort *there*
dorthin *there, thither*
der **Draht** (⸚e) *wire*
das **Drama** (Dramen) *drama*
drängen *to press, to crowd*
draußen *outside, out of doors*
dringen *to urge*
dringend *urgent, pressing*
das **Drittel** (-) *third*
drittens *thirdly*
drehen *to turn, to twist*
drohen (+dat) *to threaten*
drüben *over there*
der **Druck** (-e) *pressure, print*
drucken *to print*
drücken *to press, push*
die **Druckerei** (-en) *printing works*
die **Drucksache** *printed matter*
dumm *stupid, dull*
dunkel *dark*
die **Dunkelheit** *darkness*
dünn *thin, lean*
durch (+acc) *through, by*
durchaus *throughout, thoroughly*
durchaus nicht *by no means, not at all*
der **Durchgang** (⸚e) *passage, gateway*
dürfen *to be allowed to, may, to be likely to* (see pp. 41–42)
der **Durst** *thirst*
Durst haben *to be thirsty*
durstig *thirsty*
sich **duschen** *to take a shower*
das **Düsenflugzeug** (-e) *jet aeroplane*
das **Dutzend** (-e) *dozen*

E

eben *even, flat, level, just (of time)*

die Ebene (-n) *plain, plane*

ebenso *so, in like manner*

ebenso ... wie *just as ... as*

echt *genuine, real*

die Ecke (-n) *corner*

eckig *angular, awkward*

edel *noble*

ehe *before* (see p. 54)

eher *sooner, rather*

die Ehe (-n) *marriage*

die Ehre (-n) *honour*

ehrlich *honest(ly), honourable (ly)*

die Ehrlichkeit *honesty*

das Ei (-er) *egg*

die Eiche (-n) *oak*

der Eierkuchen (-) *omelette, pancake*

der Eifer *zeal, keenness, enthusiasm*

eifersüchtig *jealous*

eifrig *keen, eager*

eigen *own, mein eigen my own*

eigentlich *in fact, actually*

das Eigentum *property, estate*

die Eile *hurry, haste*

eilen *to hurry, hasten*

der Eilzug (⁻e) *fast (express) train*

eilig *fast*

ich habe es eilig *I'm in a hurry*

der Eimer (-) *bucket, pail*

ein(e) *one, a, an*

einander *each other, one another*

die Einbahnstraße *one-way street*

einerlei *all the same*

einfach *single, simple*

der Eingang (⁻e) *entrance*

die Einheit (-en) *unity, unit*

einheitlich *uniform*

einig *united, in agreement*

einige *some, a few*

das Einkommen (-) *income, revenue*

einladen (iv) *to invite*

die Einladung (-en) *invitation*

einmal *once, some time*

einsam *lonely*

ein-schlafen (vii) *to fall asleep*

ein-schlagen (vi) *to wrap, to enclose*

ein-schreiben (i) *to register (letters)*

einst *once (upon a time), formerly*

ein-steigen (i) *to enter (car, bus, train), get into*

ein-treten (v) *to enter (room, hall)*

der Eintritt (-) *entrance, admission*

die Eintrittskarte (-n) *(admission) ticket*

der Einwohner (-) *inhabitant*

einzeln *single*

einzig *sole, only*

das Eis *ice*

das Eisen *iron*

die Eisenbahn (-en) *railway*

elektrisch *electric*

das Element (-e) *element*

die Eltern (pl) *parents*

empfangen (vii) *to receive, to obtain*

empfehlen (iv) *to recommend*

das Ende (-n) *end*

enden *to end*

endlich *at last, in the end*

eng *narrow, tight*

die Ente (-n) *duck*

entfernt *far off, distant*

die Entfernung (-en) *distance*

entgegen (+ dat) *contrary to, against*

enthalten (vii) *to contain*

entscheiden (i) *to decide*

die Entscheidung (-en) *decision*

entschuldigen *to pardon, to excuse sb.*

sich entschuldigen *to excuse one-self, to apologize*
die Entschuldigung (-en) *excuse*
entweder . . . oder *either . . . or*
entwickeln *to develop*
der Erbe (-n) *heir*
das Erbe *inheritance*
erben *to inherit*
die Erbse (-n) *pea*
die Erde (-n) *earth, ground, soil*
sich ereignen *to happen, occur*
das Ereignis (-se) *event, occurrence, incident*
erfahren (vi) *to learn*
die Erfahrung (-en) *experience*
erfinden (iii) *to invent*
die Erfindung (-en) *invention*
der Erfolg (-e) *success*
erfolglos *unsuccessful*
erfolgreich *successful*
erfüllen *to fulfil; to carry out*
erhalten (vii) *to receive, to get*
erheblich *considerable*
sich erholen *to recover, recuperate*
erinnern *to remind*
sich erinnern an (+acc) *to remember*
die Erinnerung (-en) *remembrance, memory, souvenir*
sich erkälten *to catch cold*
die Erkältung (-en) *cold, chill*
erkennen (irr. p. 54) *to recognize, realize*
die Erkenntnis (-se) *recognition, perception*
erklären *to explain, declare*
die Erklärung (-en) *explanation*
erkranken *to become ill*
erlauben (+dat) *to permit*
die Erlaubnis (-se) *permission, licence*
erlaubt *permitted, allowed*
ernst *earnest(ly), serious(ly)*
die Ernte (-n) *harvest, crop*
erreichen *to arrive at, to reach*

der Ersatz *substitute*
erscheinen (i) *to appear, to come in sight*
erschrecken (iv) *to frighten*
sich erschrecken *to be frightened, get frightened*
erst *first, only, not until*
erstaunt *astonished, surprised*
erstens *firstly*
ertrinken (iii) *to be drowned*
erwachen (intr.) *to wake up*
erwähnen *to mention*
erwarten *to expect, to wait for, to look forward to*
erwidern *to answer, reply*
erzählen *to tell, relate*
die Erzählung (-en) *tale, story, account*
erziehen (ii) *to educate, to bring up*
die Erziehung (-en) *education, upbringing*
der Esel (-) *donkey, ass*
essen (v) *to eat*
das Essen (-) *meal, food*
der Essig (-e) *vinegar*
etwa *about, approximately*
etwas *anything, something, rather, somewhat*
ewig *eternal*
das Exemplar (-e) *copy, specimen*
der Export (-e) *export*

F

die Fabrik (-en) *factory, works, plant*
der Fabrikant (-en) *manufacturer*
das Fach (-̈er) *department, division, speciality, subject*
der Faden (-̈) *thread*
fähig *able, capable*
die Fahne (-n) *flag, banner*
die Fähre (-n) *ferry*

fahren (vi) *to travel, to ride, to drive, go* (*in vehicle*)
der **Fahrer** (-) *driver*
der **Fahrgast** (¨e) *passenger*
das **Fahrgeld** *fare*
die **Fahrkarte** (-n) *ticket*
der **Fahrplan** (¨e) *time table*
das **Fahrrad** (¨er) *bicycle*
der **Fall** (¨e) *case, incident, fall*
  fallen (vii) *to fall*
  fallen lassen *to drop*
  falls *in case, if* (see p. 54)
  falsch *false, wrong*
die **Familie** (-n) *family*
  fangen (vii) *to catch, to seize*
die **Farbe** (-n) *colour*
das **Farbfernsehen** *colour TV*
  färben *to dye, to colour*
  fast *almost*
  fassen *to hold, to contain, to grasp*
  faul *lazy, idle, rotten*
die **Faust** (¨e) *fist*
die **Feder** (-n) *feather, pen*
  fehlen (+ dat) *to be lacking, to be missing*
  Was fehlt Ihnen? *What's the matter with you?*
der **Fehler** (-) *fault, mistake*
die **Feier** (-n) *celebration, festival*
  feiern *to celebrate*
der **Feiertag** (-e) *holiday*
  fein *fine, nice*
der **Feind** (-e) *enemy*
das **Feld** (-er) *field*
der **Fels** (-en)⎱ *rock*
der **Felsen** (-)⎰
das **Fenster** (-) *window*
die **Ferien** (pl) *holidays*
  Ferien haben *to be on holiday*
  fern *distant, far*
die **Ferne** (-n) *distance*
der **Fernsehapparat** (-e) *television set*
das **Fernsehen** *television*

der **Fernsprecher** *telephone*
  fertig *ready, finished*
  fest *firm, fixed, fast*
das **Fest** (-e) *festival, celebration, party* (*social*)
  fett *fat, grease*
  feucht *damp, moist*
das **Feuer** (-) *fire*
das **Fieber** (-e) *fever*
die **Figur** (-en) *figure, form, shape*
der **Film** (-e) *film*
  finden (iii) *to find*
der **Finger** (-) *finger*
  finster *dark*
der **Fisch** (-e) *fish*
  flach *flat, smooth, even*
die **Flamme** (-n) *flame*
die **Flasche** (-n) *bottle*
das **Fleisch** *meat, flesh*
der **Fleischer** (-) *butcher*
  fleißig *industrious, hardworking*
  fliegen (ii) *to fly*
der **Flieger** (-) *pilot, aviator*
  fliehen (ii) *to flee escape*
  fließen (ii) *to flow*
  fließend *fluent(ly), running*
die **Flotte** (-n) *fleet, navy*
die **Flucht** (-en) *flight, escape*
  flüchtig *fleeting, superficial*
der **Flug** (¨e) *flight*
der **Flügel** (-) *wing*
der **Fluggast** (¨e) *air passenger*
der **Flughafen** (¨)⎱ *airport*
der **Flugplatz** (¨e)⎰
die **Flugkarte** (-n) *air ticket*
der **Flugpreis** (e) *air fare*
das **Flugzeug** (-e) *aeroplane*
der **Fluß** (Flüsse) *river*
die **Folge** (-n) *consequence, continuation, sequel*
  folgen (+ dat) *to follow, result*
  folglich *consequently*
  fordern *to demand*
die **Forderung** (-en) *demand*
  fort *away, off*

und so fort *and so on*
der Fortschritt (-e) *progress*
das Foto (s) *photograph*
die Frage (-n) *question*
fragen *to ask (for information)*
die Frau (-en) *lady, woman*
Frau 'X' *Mrs. ' X'*
das Fräulein (-) *girl, young lady*
Fräulein 'X' *Miss ' X'*
frech *impertinent, saucy, 'fresh'*
frei *free, vacant*
die Freiheit (-en) *freedom, liberty*
freilich *certainly, indeed*
freiwillig *voluntarily*
fremd *foreign, strange*
die Freude (-n) *joy, pleasure*
sich freuen *to be glad*
sich freuen auf *to look forward to*
der Freund (-e) *friend*
freundlich *friendly, kind*
der Friede (-n) *peace*
frieren (ii) *to freeze, to be very cold*
Es friert mich *I'm very cold*
frisch, *fresh, cool*
der Friseur (-e) *barber*
froh *glad, pleased*
fröhlich *cheerful, merry*
der Frost (÷e) *frost*
die Frucht (÷e) *fruit*
früh *early*
heute früh *early this morning*
morgen früh *tomorrow morning*
früher *formerly*
der Frühling (-e) *spring*
das Frühstück *breakfast*
frühstücken *to breakfast*
fühlen *to feel*
führen *to lead, guide*
der Führer (-) *leader, guide*
füllen *to fill*
der Füller (-) *fountain pen*
die Füllfeder (-n) *fountain pen*
der Funke (-n) *spark*
für (+ acc) *for*

die Furcht (-) *fear*
Furcht haben *to be afraid*
furchtbar *frightful, terrible*
fürchten *to fear, be afraid of*
der Fürst (-en) (w.n.) *prince*
das Fürstentum *principality*
die Fürstin (-nen) *princess*
der Fuß (÷e) *foot*
der Fußball *football*
der Fußgänger (-) *pedestrian*
der Fußweg (-e) *footpath, footway*

G

die Gabe (-n) *gift, present*
die Gabel (-n) *fork*
der Gang (÷e) *going, gait, pace, stroll, walk, way, gangway, passage, corridor*
ganz *whole, all, quite*
gänzlich *entirely, completely*
gar (adj) *finished, ready;* (adv) *quite, very, absolutely*
gar nicht *not at all*
die Garage (-n) *garage*
die Garderobe (-n) *cloakroom*
der Garten (÷) *garden*
das Gas (-e) *gas*
der Gast (÷e) *guest, company*
das Gasthaus (÷er) *hotel, inn*
der Gasthof (÷e) *inn, restaurant*
der Gastwirt *hotel owner, landlord*
der Gatte (-n) (w.n.) *husband*
die Gattin (-nen) *wife*
das Gebäude (-) *building*
geben (v) *to give*
Es gibt *there is, are* (see p. 43)
das Gebiet (-e) *area*
das Gebirge (-) *mountain range*
geboren *born, né(e)*
der Gebrauch (÷e) *use, custom*
die Gebrüder (*pl.*) *brothers*
die Geburt (-en) *birth*
der Geburtstag (-e) *birthday*

der **Gedanke** (-n) *thought*
das **Gedicht** (-e) *poem*
geduldig *patient*
die **Gefahr** (-en) *danger*
  Gefahr laufen *to take chances*
gefährlich *dangerous*
gefallen (+dat) *to please*
  Es gefällt ihm *He is pleased
  with it*
das **Gefühl** (-e) *feeling*
gegen (+acc) *towards, against*
die **Gegend** (-en) *area, region*
der **Gegendstand** (¨e) *subject, thing*
das **Gegenteil** (-e) *contrary*
  im Gegenteil *on the contrary*
die **Gegenwart** *presence, present
  time*
  gegenüber (+dat) *opposite,
  across*
der **Gegner** (-) *opponent, adversary*
geheim *secret*
das **Geheimnis** (-se) *secret, mystery*
gehen (viii) *to go*
  zu Fuß gehen *to walk*
  Es geht mir gut *I'm well*
das **Gehör** *hearing*
gehören (+dat) *to belong to*
die **Geige** (-n) *violin, fiddle*
geigen *to play the violin*
der **Geist** (-er) *spirit, soul, mind
  intellect, ghost, spectre*
geläufig *fluent(ly), common*
gelb *yellow*
das **Geld** (-er) *money*
der **Geldbeutel** (-) *purse*
die **Geldstrafe** *fine*
die **Gelegenheit** (-en) *opportunity,
  chance*
der **Gelehrte** (a.n.) *scholar, man of
  learning*
gelingen (iii) (+dat) *to succeed*
  Es gelingt mir *I succeed*
das **Gemälde** (-) *painting*
gemein *common, vulgar*
die **Gemeinschaft** (-en) *community*

das **Gemüse** *vegetables*
gemütlich *pleasant, cosy*
genau *exact, accurate*
der **General** (¨e) *general (army)*
genießen (ii) *to enjoy*
genug *enough*
genügend *sufficient*
der **Genuß** (**Genüsse**) *pleasure, en-
  joyment*
das **Gepäck** *luggage*
der **Gepäckraum** (¨e) *left luggage
  room*
der **Gepäckschein** (-e) *luggage
  ticket*
der **Gepäckträger** (-) *porter*
gerade *direct, straight, just*
geradeaus *straight ahead*
das **Gerät** (-e) *apparatus, instrument, gadget*
das **Geräusch** (-e) *noise*
geräuschlos *noiseless*
das **Gericht** (-e) *court (of justice)*
gering, -ste *insignificant, least*
  nicht im geringsten *not in the
  least*
gern (adv) *gladly, with pleasure*
  etwas gern haben *to like sth.*
  Er trinkt gern *He likes to drink*
der **Geruch** (¨e) *smell, aroma*
das **Gerücht** (-e) *rumour*
gesamt *whole, total*
der **Gesandte** (-n) *ambassador*
das **Geschäft** (-e) *business, store*
geschehen (v) *to happen*
das **Geschenk** (-e) *present, gift*
die **Geschichte** (-n) *story, history*
geschlossen *shut, closed*
der **Geschmack** (¨e) *taste*
geschwind *fast*
die **Geschwindigkeit** (-en) *speed*
die **Geschwister** (pl) *brothers and
  sisters*
die **Gesellschaft** (-en) *company, as-
  sociation*
das **Gesetz** (-e) *law*

das Gesicht (-er) *face*
die Gestalt (-en) *shape, form*
gestatten *to allow*
gestern *yesterday*
gesund *healthy, sound, whole-some*
die Gesundheit *health*
das Getränk (-e) *drink*
getrennt *separate*
die Gewalt (-en) *power, force, authority*
gewaltig *powerful*
das Gewehr (-e) *gun, rifle*
die Gewerkschaft (-en) *trade union*
das Gewerbe (-) *business, trade, occupation*
das Gewicht (-e) *weight*
gewinnen (iv) *to win, to gain, to earn*
gewiß *certain(ly), sure(ly)*
das Gewitter (-) *(thunder)storm*
sich gewöhnen an *to accustom one-self to*
die Gewohnheit (-en) *custom, use, habit*
gewöhnlich *usually, generally*
gießen (ii) *to pour*
das Gift (-e) *poison*
giftig *poisonous*
der Gipfel (-) *top, summit, peak*
glänzen *to shine, sparkle*
das Glas (-̈er) *glass (drinking and material)*
ein Glas Bier *a glass of beer*
glauben *to believe*
gleich (adj) *similar, same*
gleich (adv) *immediately, at once*
gleichen (+ dat) (i) *to resemble*
gleichfalls *likewise, too*
gleichgültig *indifferent, immaterial*
gleiten (i) *to glide*
das Glied (-er) *limb, part, member*
die Glocke (-n) *bell*

das Glück *happiness, good fortune*
glücklich *happy, fortunate*
glücklicherweise *fortunately*
gnädig *gracious, merciful*
gnädige Frau ⎫ *polite forms*
gnädiges Fräulein ⎭ *of address*
das Gold *gold*
der Gott (-̈er) *God.* Ach Gott! *Heavens!*
der Graben (-̈) *trench, ditch*
graben (iv) *to dig*
der Grad (-e) *degree*
der Graf (-en), die Gräfin (-nen) *Count, Countess*
die Grammatik (-en) *grammar*
das Grammophon (-e) *gramophone*
das Gras (-̈er) *grass*
gratulieren (+ dat) *to congratulate*
grau *grey*
grausam *cruel*
greifen (i) *to grasp, seize*
die Grenze (-n) *frontier, boundary*
der Griff (-e) *handle, grasp*
die Grippe *influenza*
groß, größer, größte *big, bigger, biggest*
die Größe (-n) *size, bigness*
die Großeltern (pl) *grandparents*
großmütig *generous*
die Großmutter (-̈) *grandmother*
der Großvater (-̈) *grandfather*
grün *green*
der Grund (-̈e) *ground, soil, reason, cause, motive*
gründlich *thorough*
grundlos *bottomless, unfounded*
die Gruppe (-n) *group*
der Gruß (-̈e) *greeting*
grüßen *to greet*
der Gummi (-s) *rubber, eraser*
die Gunst (-) *favour*
günstig *favourable*
gut *good*
das Gut (-̈er) *property, estate*

die Güter *goods*
die Güte *goodnesss, kindness*
das Gymnasium (ien) *(German) grammar school*

H

das Haar (-e) *hair*
sich die Haare schneiden lassen *to have one's hair cut*
haben (aux. p. 40) *to have*
Durst haben *to be thirsty*
Eile haben *to be in a hurry*
gern haben *to like*
recht haben *to be right*
unrecht haben *to be wrong*
der Hafen (:) *harbour, port*
hageln *to hail, be hailing*
der Hahn (:e) *rooster, cock, tap*
halb *half*
die Hälfte (-n) *hall, large room*
Hallo! *Hello!*
der Hals (:e) *neck, throat*
das Halstuch (:er) *scarf, muffler*
halten (vii) *to hold, to stop*
Halt! *Stop!*
die Haltestelle (-n) *halt, bus stop*
das Hammelfleisch *mutton*
der Hammer (:) *hammer, mallet*
die Hand (:e) *hand*
der Handel *trade, commerce*
handeln *to trade; do business, to bargain*
das Handgepäck *hand luggage*
der Handschuh (-e) *glove*
die Handtasche (-n) *handbag*
das Handtuch (:er) (hand) *towel*
hängen (vii) *to be hanging*
hängen (tr) *to hang sth.*
hart *hard, harsh, rough*
hassen *to hate*
häßlich *ugly*
hauen *to cut, hew, chop*
häufig *often*

das Haupt (:er) *head, chief, main (part)*
der Hauptbahnhof (:e) *main station, terminus*
der Hauptmann *captain*
die Hauptsache *main thing*
die Hauptstadt (:e) *capital, main city*
die Hauptstraße *main street, High Street*
das Haus (:er) *house*
zu Hause *at home*
nach Hause *homewards*
die Haut (:e) *skin*
heben *to lift, raise, heave*
das Heer (-e) *army*
das Heft (-e) *exercise book*
die Helde (-n) *heath, moor, heather*
heil *whole, intact*
heilig *holy, sacred*
das Heim (-e) *home*
heim (adv) *at home, home-(ward)*
die Heimat *native place, home*
Heimatdorf *native village*
Heimatland *native country*
Heimatort *native place*
Heimatstadt *native town*
die Heirat (-en) *marriage*
heiraten *to marry*
heiß *hot*
heißen (i) *to be called, mean*
Wie heißen Sie? *What's yo name?*
die Heizung (-en) *heating*
der Held (-en) (w.n.) *hero*
helfen (iv) (+ dat) *to help*
hell *bright, clear, light (of colour)*
hellrot *light red*
das Hemd (-en) *shirt*
her (adv) *to here, this way, hither*
prefix: herab *down*
heran *to (this point)*

herauf *up*
heraus *out of*
herein *in, into*
herüber *across*
herum *around*
herunter *down*
hervor *forth*
der Herbst (-e) *autumn*
der Herr (-en) *gentleman, lord* (see p. 21)
Herr 'X' *Mr. 'X'*
Herr Ober! *Waiter!*
herrlich *splendid, wonderful*
herrschen *to rule*
das Herz (-en) *heart*
heute *today*
heute abend *tonight*
heute vor acht Tagen *a week ago today*
heute in vierzehn Tagen *today fortnight*
heutzutage *now, today, nowadays*
hier *here*
die Hilfe (-n) *help*
der Himmel (-) *sky, heaven*
hin (adv) *from hence, hence, to there, thither*
hin-: hinab *down*
hinauf *up*
hinaus *out*
hindurch *through*
hinein *in, into*
hinüber *above, across*
hinunter *down*
hinzu *to*
hindern *to deter, to hinder*
das Hindernis (-se) *obstruction*
hinten (adv) *behind*
hinter (prep) (+ acc/dat) *behind, back of*
der Hintergrund *background*
hinterlassen (vii) *to leave behind*
hinüber-gehen *to cross (road)*

die Hitze *heat*
hoch *high(ly), very, exceeding-(ly)*
höchstens *at most*
die Höchstgeschwindigkeit *maximum speed*
die Hochzeit (-en) *wedding*
der Hof (⸚e) *court, courtyard, country house*
hoffen *to hope*
hoffentlich (adv) *to be hoped*
die Hoffnung (-en) *hope*
höflich *polite*
die Höhe (-n) *height*
hohl *hollow*
holen *to fetch; to go and get*
das Holz (⸚er) *wood*
der Honig *honey*
hörbar *audible*
hören *to hear*
der Hörer (-) *telephone receiver*
die Hose (-n) *pair of trousers*
das Hotel (-s) *hotel*
hübsch *pretty*
der Hügel (-) *hill*
das Huhn (⸚er) *fowl, chicken, hen*
der Humor *humour*
der Hund (-e) *dog*
hundert *hundred*
der Hunger *hunger, appetite*
Hunger haben *to be hungry*
hungrig *hungry*
husten *to cough*
der Hut (⸚e) *hat*
hüten (tr) *to watch, guard*
sich hüten vor *to beware of*
die Hütte (-n) *hut, shed, cottage*

I

illustriert *illustrated*
immer *always, ever*
in (+ acc/dat) *in, into*
indem *while, as, by* (see p. 54)

die Industrie (-n) *industry*
infolge (+ gen) *because of*
der Ingenieur (-e) *engineer*
der Inhalt (-e) *content(s)*
innen *within, inside*
innerhalb (+ gen) *inside*
das Insekt (-en) *insect*
die Insel (-n) *island*
die Intelligenz *intelligence*
intelligent *intelligent*
interessant *interesting*
sich interessieren für *to be interested in*
das Interesse *interest*
irgend(-) *some(-)*
irgendein *some . . . or other*
irgendwie *somehow*
irgendwo *somewhere*
sich irren *to be mistaken, wrong*
der Irrtum (⸚er) *error, mistake*

J

ja *yes*
die Jacke (-n) *jacket*
die Jagd (-en) *hunt, chase*
jagen *to hunt*
der Jäger (-) *hunter, huntsman*
das Jahr (-e) *year*
die Jahreszeit (-en) *season*
das Jahrhundert (-e) *century*
jährlich *yearly, annual*
jedenfalls *in any case*
jeder (e, -es) *each, every* (see p. 10)
jedermann *everybody*
je . . . desto . . . *the . . . the . . .*
je mehr desto besser *the more the better*
jedoch *however*
jemand *somebody, anybody*
jener *that, the former* (see p. 10)
jenseits (+ gen) *on that (the other) side of, beyond*

jetzt *now*
jubeln *to rejoice*
der Jude (-n) *Jew*
die Jüdin *Jewess*
jüdisch *Jewish*
die Jugend *youth*
jung *young*
die Jungfrau (-en) *virgin, spinster*
der Jüngling (-) *youth, lad, adolescent*
jüngst *recently, lately*
der Juwelier (e) *jeweller*

K

der Kaffee *coffee*
kahl *bald, bare, leafless*
der Kahn (⸚e) *skiff, boat, barge*
der Kai (-e) *quay, wharf*
die Kajüte (-n) *cabin (on ship)*
das Kalb (⸚er) *calf*
das Kalbfleisch *veal*
kalt *cold*
Mir ist kalt *I'm cold*
die Kälte *cold, coldness*
der Kamerad (-en) *comrade, pal*
der Kamin (-e) *chimney, fireside*
der Kamm (⸚e) *comb*
kämmen *to comb*
der Kampf (⸚e) *fight, struggle, match, game*
kämpfen *to fight, struggle*
der Kanal (⸚e) *canal*
die Kapelle (-n) *orchestra, chapel*
das Kapital (-ien) *capital, funds, money*
der Kapitän (-e) *captain (ship's)*
das Kapitel (-) *chapter*
kaputt *'done for', broken, finished*
die Karte (-n) *card, ticket, map*
die Kartoffel (-n) *potato*
der Käse (-) *cheese*
die Kaserne (-n) *barracks*

die **Kasse** (-n) *cash-box, cash-desk, cashier's office*

der **Kasten** (-) or (∺) *box, cupboard*

die **Katze** (-n) *cat*

kaufen *to buy*

der **Käufer** (-) *buyer*

das **Kaufhaus** (∺er) *department store*

der **Kaufmann** *businessman, merchant* (**Kaufleute**)

kaum *hardly, scarcely*

die **Kehle** (-n) *throat*

kehren *to turn, to brush, sweep*

nach Hause kehren *to return home*

kein *no, not any* (+ noun)*; none* (see p. 12)

keineswegs *not at all, by no means*

der **Keks** (e) *biscuit*

der **Kellner** (-) *waiter, steward*

die **Kellnerin** (-nen) *waitress, stewardess*

kennen (irr. p. 50) *to know (a person), to be acquainted with* (see p. 45)

die **Kenntnis** (-se) *knowledge*

der **Kerl** (-e) *fellow, chap, guy*

die **Kerze** (-n) *candle*

der **Kessel** (-) *kettle*

das **Kilogramm** (= kg) *kilogram*

der **Kilometer** (= km) *kilometer*

das **Kind** (-er) *child*

das **Kinn** (-e) *chin*

das **Kino** (-s) *cinema*

kippen *to tip*

die **Kirche** (-n) *church*

das **Kissen** (-) *pillow, cushion*

die **Klage** (-n) *complaint*

klagen (**über**) *to complain (about, of)*

klar *clear*

die **Klasse** (-n) *class*

das **Klavier** (-e) *piano*

das **Kleid** (-er) *dress, coat, garment* pl. *clothes*

sich **kleiden** *to dress oneself*

klein *small, little*

das **Kleingeld** *small change*

das **Klima** *climate*

die **Klinge** (-n) *blade*

die **Klingel** (-n) *door bell*

klingen (iii) *to sound, tinkle*

klopfen *to knock*

Es klopft *Somebody's knocking*

der **Klub** (-s) *club*

klug *wise, prudent*

der **Knabe** (-n) (w.n.) *boy*

knapp *scarce*

das **Knie** (-) *knee*

der **Knopf** (∺e) *button, stud*

der **Koch** (∺e) *cook (m)*

die **Köchin** (-nen) *cook (f)*

kochen *to cook, boil*

der **Koffer** (-) *trunk, case*

der **Kohl** *cabbage*

die **Kohle** (-n) *coal*

kolossal *colossal, huge, immense*

kommen (iv) *to come*

die **Kommode** (-n) *chest of drawers*

der **Kommunist** (-en) (w.n.) *Communist*

der **Kommunismus** *Communism*

kommunistisch (adj) *Communist*

der **König** (-e) *king*

die **Königin** (-nen) *queen*

königlich *royal*

das **Königreich** (-e) *kingdom*

können (irr. pp. 42, 50) *to be able, can*

der **Kontinent** (-e) *continent*

das **Konto** (**Konten**) *account (in bank)*

die **Kontrolle** (-n) *control, check*

das **Konzert** (-e) *concert*

der **Kopf** (∺e) *head*

das **Kopfweh** *headache*

der Korkenzieher *corkscrew*
der Körper (-) *body (living)*
der Korridor (-e) *corridor*
das Korn (¨er) *grain*
korrigieren *to correct*
die Kost (pl) (-en) *cost(s), price*
kostbar *costly, precious*
kosten *to cost*
die Kraft (¨e) *strength, force*
kräftig *strong*
der Kraftwagen (-) *motor vehicle*
das Kraftwerk *power station*
krank *ill, sick, ailing*
das Krankenhaus (¨er) *hospital*
die Krankheit (-en) *illness, disease*
die Krawatte (-n) *necktie*
die Kreide *chalk*
der Krebs (e) *cancer*
der Kreis (-e) *circle (set of people),
  ring*
der/die Krem *cream (cosmetic and
  for shoes, shaving etc.)*
das Kreuz (-e) *cross*
die Kreuzung *cross roads*
kriechen (ii) *to creep, crawl*
der Krieg (-e) *war*
kriegen *to get*
krumm *crooked, bent*
die Küche (-n) *kitchen*
der Kuchen (-) *cake*
die Kuh (¨e) *cow*
kühl *cool*
der Kühlschrank (¨e) *refrigerator*
die Kultur (-en) *culture*
der Kunde (-n) (w.n.) *customer*
künftig *in future*
die Kunst (¨e) *art*
der Künstler (-) *artist*
künstlerisch *artistic*
künstlich *artificial*
das Kupfer *copper*
der Kurs (-e) *course, rate of exchange*
die Kurve (-n) *curve, bend (on
  road)*

kurz *short, brief*
kürzlich *recently*
die Kusine (-n) *cousin (f)*
der Kuß (Küsse) *kiss*
küssen *to kiss*
die Küste (-n) *coast*

L

lachen *to laugh*
lächeln *to smile*
laden (vi) *to load*
der Laden (¨) *store, shop*
die Lage (-n) *situation, position*
das Lager (-) *camp, store-room*
lahm *lame*
die Lampe (-n) *lamp, lantern*
das Land (¨er) *land, country, pro-
  vince*
landen *to land*
die Landkarte (-n) *map*
der Landsmann (Landsleute) *countryman, fellow countryman*
die Landstraße (-n) *main road*
die Landung (-en) *landing*
der Landwirt (-e) *farmer*
die Landwirtschaft *agriculture,
  farming*
lang *long*
die Länge (-n) *length*
längs (+ gen) *along*
langsam *slow(ly)*
langweilig *tiring, boring*
der Lärm *noise*
lassen (vii) *to let, allow* (see
  p. 38)
laufen (viii) *to run*
der Laut (-e) *sound, tone*
lauten *to sound*
lauter *nothing but, only*
das Leben (-) *life*
leben *to live*
die Lebensmittel (pl) *provisions,
  food*

das **Leder** *leather*
leer *empty*
leeren *to empty, to drain*
legen *to lay, place*
lehren *to teach*
der **Lehrer** (-) *teacher, school-master*
die **Lehrerin** (-nen) *teacher* (*f*)
der **Lehrling** (-e) *apprentice*
der **Leib** (-er) *body, figure*
die **Leiche** (-n) *corpse*
leicht *easy, light*
das **Leid** *harm, wrong, sorrow*
   Es tut mir leid *I'm sorry*
das **Leiden** (-) *suffering, grief*
leiden (i) *to suffer*
leider *alas, unfortunately*
leihen (i) *to lend*
das **Leinen** (-) *linen*
leise *low (tone), soft, gentle*
   leise sprechen *to lower one's voice*
leisten *to do, to achieve*
sich **leisten** *to afford*
leiten *to guide, lead*
der **Leiter** (-) *guide, leader*
die **Lektion** (-en) *lesson*
lenken *to direct, steer*
lernen *to learn*
lesen (v) *to read*
letzt *last, final*
leuchten *to light up, illuminate*
die **Leute** (pl) *people*
das **Licht** (-er) *light*
lieb *dear*
   lieb haben *to love, like*
das **Liebchen** *darling*
die **Liebe** *love*
lieben *to love*
liebenswürdig *amiable, kind*
das **Lied** (-er) *song*
liegen (v) *to lie, rest on, be lying (on)*
die **Limonade** (-n) *lemonade*
die **Linde** (-n) *lime tree, linden*

die **Linie** (-n) *line*
   in gerader Linie *in a straight line*
links *to the left*
   links fahren *to drive on the left*
die **Lippe** (-n) *lip*
das/der **Liter** *litre*
das **Lob** *praise*
loben *to praise* (see p. 40)
das **Loch** (⁻er) *hole*
der **Löffel** (-) *spoon*
der **Lohn** (⁻e) *wage*
das **Lokal** (-e) *inn, public house*
los *loose, free*
   Was ist los? *What's happening?*
   Los! Let's go!
lösen *to loosen, solve, free* also *to buy a ticket*
der **Löwe** (-n) *lion*
die **Luft** (⁻e) *air*
die **Luftpost** *air mail*
die **Lüge** (-n) *lie, falsehood*
lügen (ii) *to lie, tell lie(s)*
die **Lust** (⁻e) *pleasure, delight*
   Lust haben *to feel disposed, inclined, fancy*
lustig *merry, jovial*

M

machen *to make*
   Es macht nichts *It doesn't matter*
die **Macht** (⁻e) *power, might*
mächtig *powerful*
das **Mädchen** (-) *girl*
der **Magen** (-) *stomach*
die **Mahlzeit** *meal*
das **Mal** (-e) *time (occasion)*
   einmal *once* ⎫ *etc.* see p. 26
   zweimal *twice*⎭
malen *to paint*
der **Maler** (-) *painter*
man *one, people, they* (see p. 32)

manch, -er, -e, -es *many (a)*
manchmal *sometimes, several times*
der Mangel (⸚) *need, want*
mangelhaft *short of, wanting*
der Mann (⸚er) *man, husband*
männlich *masculine, manly*
der Mantel (⸚) *coat, overcoat*
die Mappe (-n) *brief-case, file*
das Märchen (-) *fairy tale*
die Mark (-) *mark (German currency)*
die Marke (-n) *mark, stamp, brand*
der Markt (⸚e) *market*
der Marsch (⸚e) *march*
marschieren *to march*
die Maschine (-n) *machine*
das Maß (-e) *measure*
die Masse (-n) *mass, heap, crowd*
das Material (-en) *material*
die Mathematik *mathematics*
die Matratze (-n) *mattress*
der Matrose (-n) (w.n.) *sailor*
matt *dull, flat*
die Mauer (-n) *wall (outside)*
das Maul (⸚er) *mouth (of animals)*
die Maus (⸚e) *mouse*
der Mechaniker (-) *mechanic*
die Medizin (-en) *medicine*
das Meer (-e) *sea*
das Mehl (-) *meal, flour*
mehr *more*
mehrere *several*
mehrmals *several times*
meiden (i) *to avoid, shun*
die Meile (-n) *mile*
mein (-er, -e, -es) *my, mine* (see pp. 12, 32)
meinen *to be of opinion, to mean*
die Meinung (-en) *opinion, intention*
meist *most (of)*
am meisten *most*
meistens *mostly*

der Meister (-) *master*
melden *to report, to give notice of*
die Meldung (-en) *report, notice*
die Melodie (-n) *melody*
die Menge (-n) *crowd*
der Mensch (-en) (w.n.) *human being, man*
merken *to notice*
merkwürdig *strange*
messen (v) *to measure*
das Messer (-) *knife*
das Messing *brass*
das Metall (-e) *metal*
das/der Meter (-) *metre (39 in.)*
die Miete (-n) *rent*
mieten *to rent, to hire*
die Milch *milk*
militärisch *military*
die Million (-en) *million*
minder *less*
mindestens *at least*
das Mineral (-e) *mineral*
das Mineralwasser *mineral water*
der Minister (-) *minister (of govt.)*
die Minute (-n) *minute*
das Mißverständnis (-se) *misunderstanding*
mit (+ dat) *with*
das Mitglied (-er) *member, associate*
das Mitleid *sympathy*
der Mitreisende (a.n.) *fellow-traveller*
der Mittag *midday, noon*
das Mittagessen *midday meal, lunch(eon)*
die Mitte (-n) *middle, centre*
das Mittel *means*
mitten *amongst*
mitten in der Stadt *in the middle of the town*
die Mitternacht *midnight*
das Möbel (-) *(piece of) furniture*
die Mode (-n) *fashion*

modisch *fashionable*
mögen *to like to, may* (see pp. 42, 50)
möglich *possible*
der Moment (-e) *moment*
der Monat (-e) *month*
monatlich *monthly*
der Mond (-e) *moon*
der Mord (-e) *murder*
morden *to murder*
der Mörder (-) *murderer*
der Morgen (-) *morning*
morgen *tomorrow*
morgen früh *tomorrow morning*
das Motorrad (⸚er) *motorcycle*
müde *tired*
die Mühe (-n) *trouble, difficulty*
Es ist nicht der Mühe wert *It's not worth the trouble*
der Mund (⸚er) *mouth (of person)*
die Mündung (-en) *mouth (of river)*
das Münster (-) *cathedral, minster*
munter *cheerful, lively*
das Museum (Museen) *museum*
die Musik *music*
der Musiker (-) *musician*
der Muskel (-n) *muscle*
müssen *to have to, must* (see pp. 42, 50)
das Muster (-) *pattern, sample*
müßig *idle*
der Mut *spirit, courage*
Mut haben *to be brave*
die Mutter (⸚) *mother*
die Mütze (-n) *cap, bonnet*

N

nach (+ dat) *after, towards, to*
der Nachbar (-n) (w.n.) *neighbour*
nachdem *after* (see p. 54)
nachher *afterwards, by and by*
nachlässig *careless*
der Nachmittag (-e) *afternoon*

nachmittags *in the afternoon*
die Nachricht (-en) *news*
nächst *next, nearest*
nächstens *shortly, soon*
die Nacht (⸚e) *night*
das Nachtlokal (-e) *night club*
die Nadel (-n) *needle, pin*
der Nagel (⸚) *nail, tack*
nahe (+ dat) *near*
die Nähe *vicinity, nearness*
in der Nähe *near*
nähen *to sew*
sich nähern (+ dat) *to approach*
nähren *to nourish*
die Nahrung *food, nourishment*
der Name (-n) (w.n.) *name*
nämlich *namely, you see*
die Nase (-n) *nose*
naß *wet*
die Nation (-en) *nation*
national *national*
die Nationalität *nationality*
die Natur (-en) *nature*
natürlich *natural(ly), of course*
der Nebel (-) *fog, mist*
neben (+ acc/dat) *beside, near*
neblig *foggy, misty*
der Neffe (-n) (w.n.) *nephew*
der Neger (-) *Negro*
die Neigung (-en) *inclination, tendency*
nehmen (iv) *to take*
nein *no*
nennen (irr. p. 50) *to name*
nett *pleasant, nice*
das Netz (-e) *net*
neu *new*
das Neujahr *New Year*
neulich *the other day, recently*
nicht *not*
überhaupt nicht *not at all*
die Nichte (-n) *niece*
der Nichtraucher (-) *non-smoker (person, carriage on train)*
nichts *nothing, not anything*

nie *never*
nieder *down*
niedrig *low, insignificant, base*
niemals *never*
niemand *nobody*
nirgends *nowhere*
noch *yet, still*
noch nicht *not yet*
der Norden *north*
nördlich *northern*
die Nordsee *North Sea*
die Not (ːe) *need, necessity*
die Notbremse (-n) *emergency brake*
die Note (-n) *note (in music, money)*
nötig *needful, necessary*
notwendig *necessary, required*
die Null (-en) *zero, nought, nonentity*
nun (adv) *now*, (conj) *Well!*
Nun gut! *All right! O.K.*
nur *only*
die Nuß (Nüsse) *nut*
der Nutzen *use, profit*
nützen *to be of use*
das nützt mir gar nichts *that's no use at all to me*
nützlich *useful*
nutzlos *useless*

O

ob *if, whether* (see p. 54)
oben (adv) *above, upstairs*
Ober, Herr Ober! *Waiter!*
ober (adj and prefix) *upper, higher, principal, head, chief*
der Oberkellner (-) *head waiter*
der Oberst (-en) *colonel*
obgleich ⎱
obwohl ⎰ *although* (see p. 54)
das Obst *fruit*
der Obstgarten (ː) *orchard*
der Ochse (-n) (w.n.) *ox, bullock*
oder *or*

der Ofen (ː) *stove, oven, furnace*
offen *open*
offentlich *public, open*
der Offizier (-e) *officer*
öffnen *to open*
die Öffnung (-en) *opening*
oft *often*
ohne (+ acc) *without*
ohne Zweifel *no doubt*
ohnmächtig *fainting, powerless*
ohnmächtig werden *to faint*
das Ohr (-en) *ear*
das Öl *oil*
der Omnibus (-se) *omnibus, bus*
der Onkel (-) *uncle*
die Oper (-n) *opera*
das Opernhaus (ːer) *opera house*
das Opfer (-) *victim, sacrifice*
das Orchestra (-) *orchestra*
ordentlich *thoroughly, properly, decent*
ordnen *to put in order, arrange*
die Ordnung (-en) *arrangement, order, rule*
die Orgel (-n) *organ*
der Ort (-e) *place*
der Osten *east*
das Ostern *Easter*
östlich *eastern*
die Ostsee *Baltic Sea*
der Ozean (-e) *ocean*

P

das Paar (-e) *pair, couple, brace*
ein Paar Schuhe *a pair of shoes*
ein paar *a few*
ein paar Worte *a few words*
ein paar Stunden, Tage, Monate *a few hours, days, months, etc.*
packen *to pack*
das Paket (-e) *parcel*
der Palast (ːe) *palace*

die **Panne** (-n) *puncture, breakdown*
  ein Panne haben *to have a
  breakdown (of a car)*
das **Papier** (-e) *paper*
der **Papst** (⸚e) *pope*
der **Park** (-e or -s) *park*
  parken *to park*
der **Parkplatz** (⸚e) *parking place,
  car park*
die **Partei** (-en) *political party*
das **Parterre** *pit (in a theatre),
  ground floor*
der **Paß** (Pässe) *passport, permit,
  pass*
  passen (+ dat) *to suit, to fit*
  passieren *to happen*
die **Paste** (-n) *paste*
  or Pasta
der **Patient** (-en) (w.n.) *patient*
die **Pause** (-n) *pause, interval, rest*
der **Pelz** (-e) *fur*
die **Pension** (-en) *boarding house*
die **Person** (-en) *person, individual*
die **Personenzug** (⸚e) *slow passenger train*
  persönlich *personally*
der **Pfad** (-e) *path*
der **Pfandfinder** (-) *boy scout*
die **Pfadfinderin** (-nen) *girl guide*
die **Pfanne** (-n) *pan*
der **Pfeffer** *pepper*
  pfeifen (i) *to whistle*
der **Pfennig** (-e) *100 = 1 Mark*
das **Pferd** (-e) *horse*
das **Pferderennen** *horse-racing*
das **Pfingsten** *Whitsuntide*
der **Pfingstsonntag** *Whit Sunday*
der **Pfingstmontag** *Whit Monday*
die **Pflanze** (-n) *plant (botany)*
  pflanzen *to plant, implant*
die **Pflaume** (-n) *plum*
die **Pflege** (-n) *care, looking-after,
  management*
  pflegen *to be in the habit of, to
  nurse, take care of*

die **Pflicht** (-en) *duty*
  pflücken *to pick*
der **Pflug** (⸚e) *plough*
das **Pfund** (-e) *pound (lb. and £)*
die **Philosophie** (-n) *philosophy*
der **Photograph** (-en) (w.n.) *photo-
  grapher*
die **Photographie** (-n) *photography*
  photographieren *to photograph,
  take a photograph*
die **Pille** (-n) *pill*
der **Pilz** (-e) *mushroom, fungus*
der **Pinsel** *brush (for painting, shaving)*
der **Plan** (⸚e) *plan*
der **Planet** (-en) (w.n.) *planet*
die **Plastik** (-en) *plastic art, plastic*
  platt *flat*
die **Platte** (-n) *record, disc*
  plätten *to iron, press*
der **Plattenspieler** (-) *record player*
der **Platz** (⸚e) *place, seat, space,
  square*
  Platz nehmen *to sit down*
  plötzlich *sudden(ly)*
  politisch *political*
die **Polizei** (-en) *police*
der **Polizist** (-en) (w.n.) *policeman*
die **Polizeistunde** (-n) *closing time
  (in drinking places)*
der **Portier** (-s) *hall porter (hotel),
  caretaker*
das **Porto** *postage*
  Das Porto beträgt ... *The postage is ...*
die **Post** *post, post office, mail*
das **Postamt** (⸚er) *post office*
die **Postkarte** (-n) *post card*
  praktisch *practical*
der **Präsident** (-en) *president, chair-
  man* (w.n.)
der **Preis** (-e) *price, prize*
die **Presse** (-n) *press*
  privat *private*
der **Privatweg** (-e) *private road*

die **Probe** (-n) *test, try-out, trial, rehearsal, sample, pattern*
  auf Probe *on probation, trial*
das **Produkt** (-e) *product*
das **Programm** (-e) *programme*
das **Prozent** (-e) *per cent, percentage*
der **Prozeß** (**Prozesse**) *law suit, trial*
  prüfen *to test, examine*
das **Publikum** *public*
die **Prüfung** (-en) *examination, test*
der **Puder** (-) *powder*
der **Pulli** (-s) *pullover, sweater*
der **Punkt** (-e) *point, dot, full stop*
  pünktlich *punctual*
die **Puppe** (-n) *doll*
  putzen *to polish, shine, clean*

Q

  quälen *to torture, torment*
die **Quantität** *quantity*
der **Quatsch** *foolish talk, nonsense*
  Das is alles Quatsch *That's a load of rubbish*
die **Quelle** (-n) *spring, well, source*
  quellen (ii) *to spring from, start from*
  quer *slanting, across*
  quer durch *right through, across*

R

  die **Rache** *revenge*
sich rächen an *to get revenge on*
  das **Rad** (:er) *wheel, bicycle*
der **Radfahrer** (-) *cyclist*
der **Radiergummi** (-s) *rubber, eraser*
das **Radio** (-s) *radio*
der **Rahm** *cream*
der **Rand** (:er) *edge, brim*
  rasch *rapid(ly), quick(ly)*
sich rasieren *to shave (oneself)*

der **Rasierapparat** (-e) *razor*
die **Rasierklinge** (-n) *razor blade*
die **Raststätte** (-n) *resting place*
  rasten *to take a rest*
der **Rat** (pl. die **Ratschläge**) *advice, council, councillor*
  raten (vii) (+ dat) *to advise, guess*
das **Rathaus** (:er) *town hall*
das **Rätsel** (-) *riddle, puzzle*
die **Ratte** (-n) *rat*
  rauben *to rob, steal*
der **Räuber** *robber*
der **Rauch** *smoke*
  rauchen *to smoke*
der **Raucher** (-) *smoker (person and carriage)*
der **Raum** (:e) *room, space*
  rechnen *to reckon, calculate*
die **Rechnung** (-en) *bill, invoice, account*
das **Recht** (-e) *law, privilege, right*
  recht *right, correct*
  rechts *to the right.*—**fahren** *to drive on the right*
die **Rede** (-n) *speech, talk*
  reden *to speak, talk*
der **Redner** (-) *speaker, orator*
die **Regel** (-n) *rule*
der **Regen** (-) *rain*
der **Regenschirm** (-e) *umbrella*
die **Regierung** (-en) *government, regime*
  regnen *to rain*
  reich *rich*
das **Reich** (-e) *empire, kingdom*
  reichen *to reach, to hand*
der **Reichtum** (:er) *riches, wealth*
  reif *ripe, mature*
  reifen *to ripen, mature*
der **Reifen** (-) *tyre*
die **Reihe** (-n) *row, line, series, turn, rank*
  Die Reihe ist an mir *It's my turn*
  rein *clean*

reinigen *to clean*
die Reise (-n) *journey, voyage*
reisen *to travel*
der/die Reisende (a.n.) *traveller*
reiten (i) *to ride (on horseback)*
der Reiz (-e) *charm,* also *irritation*
reizen *to charm, provoke, irritate*
reizend *charming*
die Religion (-en) *religion*
rennen (irr. p. 50) *to run*
die Republik (-en) *republic*
reservieren *to reserve*
das Restaurant (-s) *restaurant*
retten *to rescue, save*
der Retter (-) *rescuer, saviour*
die Rettung (-en) *rescue, salvage*
die Reue *repentance, regret*
das Rezept (-e) *prescription, recipe*
richten *to direct, to judge*
der Richter (-) *judge*
richtig *right, correct*
die Richtung (-en) *direction*
riechen (ii) *to smell*
die Rinde *rind, bark (of tree), peel*
das Rindfleisch *beef*
das Rindvieh *cattle*
der Ring (-e) *ring, circle*
der Rock (̈e) *man's coat, skirt*
der Rhein *the river Rhine*
roh *raw, brutal*
das Rohr (-e) *tube, reed*
die Rollbahn (-en) *runway*
die Rolle (-n) *role, reel, roll*
der Roller (-) *scooter*
der Roman (-e) *novel*
die Rose (-n) *rose*
rot *red*
rötlich *reddish*
die Rübe *beet*
die gelbe Rübe *carrot*
die rote Rübe *beetroot*
die weiße Rübe *turnip*
die Zuckerrübe *sugar beet*
der Rücken (-) *back, ridge*

rückwärts *backwards*
der Rückweg (-e) *way back, way home*
das Ruder (-) *oar*
das Ruderboot (-e) *rowing boat*
rudern *to row*
der Ruf (-) *call, shout, cry*
rufen (viii) *to call (out), shout*
die Ruhe *rest, peace*
ruhen *to rest*
ruhig *calm, quite, serene*
der Ruhm *honour, glory, renown*
rühmen *to praise*
das Rührei (-er) *scrambled egg*
rund *round, circular*
der Rundfunk *broadcasting (radio)*
der Rundfunksender *radio station, transmitter*
die Rundfunksendung (-en) *broadcast*
rüstig *vigorous, active*
die Rüstung (-en) *equipment, armament*

S

der Saal (Säle) *large room, hall*
die Sache (-n) *thing, matter, subject*
Meine Sache *my business*
der Sack (̈e) *sack, bag*
die Sage (-n) *legend, tale*
sagen *to say, tell*
die Sahne *cream (of milk)*
der Salat (-e) *salad, lettuce*
das Salz (-e) *salt*
der Samen (-) *seed, semen*
sammeln *to gather, collect*
die Sammlung (-en) *collection*
samt (+ dat) *together with*
der Sand (-e) *sand*
sanft *soft, gentle, mild*
der Sänger (-) *singer*

satt *tired of, sick of, satiated, full*

sättigen *to satisfy*

der Satz (¨e) *sentence (in prose)*

sauber *tidy, clean*

sauer *sour*

schade (adj) **Wie schade!** *What a pity!*

schaden *to damage, hurt*

der Schaden (¨) *damage, harm*

schädlich *harmful*

das Schaf (-e) *sheep*

schaffen *to do, work*

schaffen (vi) *to create*

der Schaffner (-) *guard (of train), conductor (of bus)*

der Schall (-e) *sound*

die Schallplatte (-n) *record (gramophone)*

schalten *to switch, change gear*

der Schalter (-) *ticket office, switch*

das Schaltjahr (-e) *leap year*

sich schämen (+ gen) *to be ashamed of*

die Schande *shame, disgrace*

die Schar (-en) *crowd, pack, herd*

scharf *sharp, keen*

der Schatten (-) *shade, shadow*

schattig *shady*

der Schatz (¨e) *treasure, darling*

schätzen *to treasure, value, estimate*

schaudern *to shudder*

schauen *to look*

das Schaufenster *shop window, display window*

der Schaum (¨e) *froth, foam*

schäumen *to froth, foam*

der Scheck (-s) *cheque*

die Scheibe (-n) *slice, pane (of glass)*

scheiden (i) *to separate, to part*

der Schein *shining, light*, also *appearance, and ticket, chit*

scheinen (i) *to seem, to shine*

schelten (iv) *to scold*

die Schenke (-n) *tavern*

schenken *to give (as a present)*

die Schere (-n) *pair of shears, scissors*

scherzen *to joke, jest*

scherzhaft *joking, jesting*

der Schi ⎫ *(Skier) ski, skis*
Ski ⎭

schi-(ski-)laufen *to ski*

schicken *to send*

das Schicksal (-e) *fate, destiny*

schieben (ii) *to shove, push*

schief *sloping, slanting*

schief gehen *to go wrong, off the rails*

schießen (ii) *to shoot*

das Schiff (-e) *ship, boat*

das Schild (-er) *signboard, plaque*

der Schinken (-) *ham*

der Schirm (-e) *shield, protection, screen, umbrella*

die Schlacht (-en) *battle, fight*

schlachten *to slaughter, kill*

der Schlaf *sleep*

der Schlafanzug (¨e) *pyjamas*

schlafen (vii) *to sleep*

der Schlafrock (¨e) *dressing-gown*

der Schlafwagen (-) *sleeping car train*

der Schlag (¨e) *blow*

schlagen (vi) *to hit, strike, beat*

die Schlagsahne *whipped cream*

die Schlagzeile (-n) *headline (newspaper)*

die Schlange (-n) *queue, snake*

Schlange stehen *to queue*

schlank *slim, slender*

schlau *sly, cunning*

schlecht *bad, evil*

schlicht *simple, plain, smooth*

schließen (ii) *to lock, close, shut*

der Schlitten (-) *sledge, toboggan*

der Schlittschuh (e) *skate*

Schlittschuh laufen *to skate*

das Schloß (Schlösser) *castle, lock*
schlummern *to slumber, sleep*
der Schluß (Schlüsse) *end, conclusion*
der Schlüssel (-) *key*
schmal *narrow*
schmecken *to taste*
schmeicheln *to falter*
der Schmerz (-en) *pain, ache, grief*
schmerzen *to pain, to grieve*
schmerzhaft *painful(ly), sore(ly)*
der Schmuck *ornament, jewellery*
sich schminken *to put on make-up*
schmutzig *dirty, filthy, nasty*
der Schnaps (ⸯe) *brandy, spirits*
der Schnee *snow*
schneiden (i) *to cut*
der Schneider (-) *tailor, cutter*
schneien *to snow*
schnell *quick(ly), rapid(ly)*
der Schnellzug (ⸯe) *express train*
der Schnupfen (-) *common cold*
die Schnur (ⸯe) *string, cord, lace*
die Schokolade (-n) *chocolate*
schon *already, in time, now, indeed*
schön *beautiful, handsome, fine*
die Schönheit *beauty*
der Schrank (ⸯe) *cupboard*
der Schrecken (-) *terror, fright*
schrecklich *terrible, frightful*
der Schrei (-e) *call, cry, scream*
schreiben (i) *to write*
die Schreibmaschine (-n) *typewriter*
schreien (i) *to cry out, shout*
schreiten *to stride, step*
die Schrift (-en) *writing*
schriftlich *in writing, in black and white*
der Schrift (-e) *step, pace*
der Schuh (-e) *shoe*
der Schuhmacher (-) *shoemaker*
die Schuld (-en) *debt, fault, guilt*
schuldig *guilty*
schuldig sein (+ dat) *to owe*

die Schule (-n) *school*
der Schüler (-) *schoolboy*
die Schülerin (nen) *schoolgirl*
die Schulter (-n) *shoulder*
der Schuster (-) *cobbler, shoe-repairer*
der Schuß (Schüsse) *shot*
schütteln *to shake*
der Schutz *protection, shelter*
schützen *to protect, shelter, guard*
der Schutzman *policeman*
schwach *weak, feeble*
die Schwäche (-n) *weakness*
der Schwager (ⸯ) *brother-in-law*
die Schwägerin (-nen) *sister-in-law*
der Schwamm (ⸯe) *sponge*
der Schwanz (ⸯe) *tail*
schwarz *black*
der Schwarzwald *Black Forest*
schweigen (i) *to be silent, to hold one's tongue*
das Schweigen *silence*
das Schwein (-e) *pig*
die Schweinerei (-en) *filth, nastiness*
das Schweinefleisch *pork*
schwellen (ii) *to swell*
schwer *heavy, difficult*
schwermütig *dejected, sad*
die Schwester (-n) *sister*
schwierig *difficult*
die Schwierigkeit (-en) *difficulty*
schwimmen (iv) *to swim*
schwitzen *to sweat, perspire*
schwören *to swear, to take an oath*
der See (-n) *lake*
die See *sea*
die Seekrankheit *sea sickness*
die Seele (-n) *soul*
die Seereise (-n) *sea voyage*
sehen (v) *to see*
sich sehnen (nach) *to long for*
sehr *very*

die Seife (-n) *soap*
sein *to be* (see pp. 40, 45)
seit (prep + dat, conj) *since* (see pp. 52, 54)
seitdem (conj) *since* (see p. 54)
die Seite (-n) *side, page*
seither *since then*
der Sekretär (-e) *secretary, clerk*
die Sekretärin (-nen) *secretary*
der Sekt (-e) *champagne*
selbst *self, even*
ich selbst *I myself etc.*
selbständig *independent*
selbstlos *unselfish*
selten *seldom, rare*
seltsam *strange, odd*
das Semester (-) *school or university term*
senden (irr. p. 50) *to send, despatch, to broadcast*
der Sender (-) *radio transmitter*
die Sendung (-en) *transmission, broadcast, consignment*
der Senf (-e) *mustard*
separat *separate*
der Sessel (-) *easy chair*
setzen *to set, to put, to place*
sich setzen *to sit down*
sich *self* (reflexive pronoun)
sicher *safe, sure, certain*
sichtbar *visible, evident*
der Sieg (-e) *victory, triumph*
das Silber *silver*
singen (iii) *to sing*
sinken (iii) *to sink*
der Sinn (-e) *sense, mind*
sitzen (v) *to sit*
der Ski *see der Schi*
die Skizze (-n) *sketch*
skizzieren *to sketch*
so *thus, in this way, so*
So! *Indeed! So so! pretty well*
Sowieso ... *In any case*
So oder so *In one way or another*

Wieso? *How so?*
Sobald ... *As soon as*
so daß *so that*
die Socke (-n) *sock*
das Sodawasser *soda water*
das Sofa (-s) *sofa*
soeben *just*
sofort *immediately, at once*
sogar *even*
sogleich *immediately, at once*
der Sohn (¨e) *son*
solch (-er, e, -es) *such*
Ein solcher Mann *such a man*
der Soldat (-en) (w.n.) *soldier*
sollen *to be obliged to, must, ought to* (see pp. 41-2, 50)
der Sommer (-) *summer*
die Sonderausgabe *special edition (of newspaper, book)*
der Sonderzug (¨e) *special train*
sonderbar *strange, singular, odd*
sondern (conj) *but*
die Sonne (-n) *sun*
der Sonnenschein *sunshine*
der Sonnenschirm (-e) *parasol*
sonst *or, else, otherwise*
die Sorge (-n) *care, anxiety, sorrow*
sorgen *to care for*
sich sorgem um *to be anxious about*
sorgfältig *careful*
soviel (wie) *as much (as)*
sowohl als *as well as*
sparen *to save, to economize*
der Spargel (-) *asparagus*
der Spaß (¨e) *joke, jest*
spaßhaft *joking(ly)*
spät *late*
der Spatz (-en) *sparrow*
spätestens *at the latest*
spazieren gehen *to walk, to go for a walk*
der Spaziergang *walk*
der Speck (-e) *bacon*

die Speise (-n) *food*
die Speisekarte (-n) *menu*
der Speisesaal ⎫
das Speisezimmer⎭ *dining room*
  speisen *to dine*
der Speisewagen (-) *dining car (train)*
die Spesen *expenses, charges*
der Spiegel (-) *looking-glass, mirror*
das Spiel (-e) *game, play*
  spielen *to play*
der Spieler (-) *player, gambler*
der Spielplatz *play ground*
der Spinat (-e) *spinach*
  spinnen (iv) *to spin, to purr (of cat)*
der Spion (-e) *spy*
  spitz *pointed*
die Spitze (-n) *point, top, tip*
der Sport *sport*
die Sprache (-n) *language*
  sprechen (iv) *to speak*
  springen (iii) *to jump*
  spülen *to wash, rinse, clean*
  spucken *to spit*
die Spur (-en) *track, vestige, trace*
der Staat (-en) *the State*
die Stadt (-̈e) *town, city*
der Stahl *steel*
der Stamm (-̈e) *stem, trunk (of tree), stock, race*
der Stand (-̈e) *stand, standing place, station, position, rank*
  stark *strong*
die Stärke (-n) *strength, power*
  statt (+ gen) *instead of*
  stattfinden *to take place, happen*
  stattlich *stately, imposing, handsome*
der Staub *dust*
der Staubsauger *vacuum cleaner*
  staubig *dusty*
  staunen über *to be astonished at*
  stecken *to stick, pin, put*

die Stecknadel (-n) *pin*
  stehen (irr. p. viii) *to stand*
  stehlen (iv) *to steal*
  steif *stiff*
  steigen (i) *to mount, go up*
  steil *steep*
der Stein (-e) *stone*
die Stelle (-n) *spot, place*
  stellen *to put, place, to set (a clock)*
die Stellung (-en) *situation, position*
der Stempel (-) *(rubber) stamp*
  sterben (iv) *to die*
der Stern (-e) *star*
  stets *always*
die Steuer (-n) *tax, duty, rate*
der Stiefel (-) *boot*
  still *calm, quiet*
die Stimme (-n) *voice, vote*
  stimmen *to sound, to put in, to vote*
die Stimmung (-en) *mood, disposition, humour*
  stinken (iii) *to stink*
die Stirne (-n) *brow, forehead*
der Stock (-̈e) *stick, storey (of house)*
der Stoff (-e) *cloth, stuff, substance*
  stolz auf *proud of*
der Stolz *pride*
  stören *to disturb*
die Störung *disturbance*
  stoßen (viii) *to push*
die Strafe (-n) *punishment*
  strafen *to punish*
der Strand (-e) *strand, beach*
die Straße (-n) *street*
die Straßenbahn (-en) *tram, streetcar*
  streichen (i) *to strike, spread, paint*
das Streichholz (-̈er) *match*
der Streik (-s) *strike*
der Streit (-e) *dispute, struggle, quarrel*

streiten (i) *to dispute, argue about, to disagree*
streng *severe*
der Strich (-e) *stroke, dash*
der Strom (¨e) *stream, river, current (and of electricity)*
strömen *to flow*
die Strömung (-en) *current (of river)*
der Strumpf (¨e) *stocking*
die Stube (-n) *room, chamber*
das Stück *bit, piece, fragment*
der Student (-en) (w.n.) *student*
studieren *to study*
das Studium (-ien) *study, pursuit of*
der Stuhl (¨e) *chair*
stumm *dumb, silent*
stumpf *blunt, dull*
die Stunde (-n) *hour (60 minutes)*
stündlich *hourly*
der Sturm (¨e) *storm*
stützen *to support*
suchen *to seek, search, look for*
der Süden *south*
südlich *southern*
die Suppe (-n) *soup*
süß *sweet*
die Symphonie (-n) *symphony*
das Symptom (-e) *symptom*
synthetisch *synthetic*

T

der Tabak (-e) *tobacco*
die Tabakhandlung (-en) *tobacconist's*
der Tadel (-) *blame*
tadelos *blameless*
tadeln *to blame*
die Tafel *(black)board, table, chart*
der Tag (-e) *day*
täglich *daily*
das Tal (¨er) *valley*
die Tanne (-n) *fir*

die Tante (-n) *aunt*
der Tanz (¨e) *dancing, dance*
tanzen *to dance*
tapfer *brave*
die Tasche (-n) *pocket*
das Taschenbuch (¨er) *paper-back (book)*
das Taschentuch (¨er) *handkerchief*
die Taschenuhr (-en) *pocket watch*
das Taschenwörterbuch *pocket dictionary*
die Tasse (-n) *cup*
Ober- und Untertasse *cup and saucer*
die Tat (-en) *deed, act, action*
tätig *active, busy*
die Tätigkeit (-en) *activity*
die Tatsache (-n) *fact, matter of fact*
der Tau *dew*
taub *deaf*
tauchen *to dive*
taugen *to be of use, fit for*
tauschen *to exchange, 'swop'*
das Tauwetter *thaw*
das Taxi (-s) *taxi*
die Technik (-en) *technology*
technisch *technical*
der Tee *tea*
eine Tasse Tee *a cup of tea*
der Teil (-) *part, share, portion*
teilen *to divide, separate, share*
teil-nehmen (an) (iv) *to take part (in); share (in)*
teils *in part*
das Telegramm (-e) *telegram*
telegraphieren *to telegraph, send a telegram*
das Telefon (-e) *telephone*
telephonieren *to telephone*
der Teller (-) *plate*
die Temperatur (-en) *temperature*
das Tennis *tennis*
der Teppich (-e) *rug, carpet*
der Termin (-e) *term, appointed day*

das **Testament** (-e) *last will, testament*

teuer *dear, costly, expensive*

der **Teufel** (-) *devil*

das **Theater** (-) *theatre*

das **Thermometer** *thermometer*

tief *deep, profound*

die **Tiefe** (-n) *depth(s)*

das **Tier** (-e) *animal*

der **Tiergarten** (⸚e) *zoological gardens, zoo*

die **Tinte** (-n) *ink*

der **Tisch** (-) *table*

das **Tischtuch** (⸚er) *table cloth*

die **Tochter** (⸚) *daughter*

der **Tod** (-e) *death*

die **Toilette** (-n) *toilet, W.C.*

der **Ton** (⸚e) *sound, tone*

der **Topf** (⸚e) *pot, jar*

das **Tor** (-e) *gate, goal, (football)*

tot *dead*

töten *to kill*

tödlich *fatal(ly), mortal(ly)*

der **Tourist** (-en) (w.n.) *tourist*

tragen (vi) *to carry, to wear*

die **Träne** (-n) *tear*

der **Transport** (-e) *transport*

die **Traube** (-n) *grape*

trauen (+ dat) *to trust*

der **Traum** (⸚e) *dream*

träumen *to dream*

träumerisch *dreamy, fanciful*

traurig *sad*

treffen (iv) *to meet, hit, strike*

treiben (i) *to drive, force, carry on*

trennen *to separate*

die **Treppe** (-n) *staircase, steps*

treten (v) *to step, tread*

treu *true, faithful*

die **Treue** *fidelity, faithfulness*

trinken (iii) *to drink*

das **Trinkgeld** (-er) *tip, gratuity*

trocken *dry, dried up, withered*

der **Tropfen** (-) *drop*

trotz (+ gen) *in spite of*

der **Trotz** *defiance; spite*

trotzdem *however*

trotzen (+ dat) *to defy*

trüb *dim, gloomy, muddy*

die **Trümmer** (pl) *fragments, ruins*

die **Truppe** (-n) *troop(s)*

das **Tuch** (-e) *cloth*

die **Tür** (-en) *door*

tun (tat, getan) *to do*

Es tut mir leid *I'm sorry*

Es tut weh *It hurts*

der **Turm** (⸚e) *tower*

das **Turnen** *gymnastics*

U

übel *wrong(ly), bad(ly)*

üben *to practise, to exercise*

über (prep and adv) (+ acc/dat) (also common prefix) *above, over, by, via, beyond, about, on, super-*

über-gehen (viii) *to cross over*

überall *everywhere*

der **Übergang** *crossing, transition*

überhaupt *in general, in all, at all*

überhaupt nicht *not at all*

überlassen (vii) *to leave, give up, give way to*

überlegen *to reflect, to consider*

die **Überlegung** (-en) *consideration*

übermorgen *day after tomorrow*

übernachten *to stay the night*

übernehmen (iv) *to take over*

überraschen *to surprise*

die **Überraschung** (-en) *surprise*

überreden *to persuade*

übersehen (v) *to overlook*

übersetzen *to translate*

der **Übersetzer** (-) *translator*

die **Übersetzung** (-en) *translation*

überwältigen *to overpower*

überzeugen *to convince, persuade*

übrig *left over, surplus*

Ich habe nichts dafür übrig *I have no use for that*

die Übung (-en) *practice, exercise*

das Ufer (-) *shore, beach, bank of river*

die Uhr (-en) *watch, clock, time of day*

Wieviel Uhr ist es? *What time is it?*

Es ist ein Uhr, zwei Uhr *It's one, two o'clock* (see p. 26)

der Uhrmacher (-) *watchmaker*

um (prep + acc and adv; also sep. prefix) *round, roundabout, gone by*

um zu *in order to*

umarmen *to embrace*

umfassend *comprehensive, extensive*

umgeben (v) *to surround*

die Umgebung (-en) *surroundings, environs*

umgehen *to escape, to go round*

um-kehren *to turn round*

der Umschlage (-̈e) *envelope*

umsonst *in vain, free of charge*

der Umstand (-̈e) *circumstance,* (pl) *particulars, details*

ohne Umstände *without fuss, ceremony*

um-steigen *to change trains*

der Umweg (-e) *detour, roundabout way*

um-ziehen (ii) *to remove, move house*

un- (prefix) *the contrary, not so much (of)*

unartig *badly behaved, naughty*

unbegründet *unfounded, unjustified*

unbekannt *unknown*

unbescheiden *immodest, impudent, rude*

unbeschreiblich *indescribable*

unbestimmt *undecided, indefinite, vague*

und *and*

unendlich *endless, infinite*

unerträglich *unbearable*

der Unfall (-̈e) *accident*

unfreundlich *unfriendly*

die Ungeduld *impatience*

ungeduldig *impatient*

ungefähr *about, approximately*

ungeheuer *huge, immense*

ungestört *undisturbed*

das Unglück (-e) *misfortune, accident*

unglücklich *unhappy, unlucky, unfortunate*

unhöflich *impolite*

die Uniform (-en) *uniform*

die Union (-en) *union*

die Universität (-en) *university*

unmöglich *impossible*

unrecht *wrong, unjust*

Ich habe unrecht *I'm wrong*

unreif *unripe*

unsichtbar *invisible*

unten *below, downstairs*

unter (prep + acc/dat and sep prefix) *under, beneath, below, between, amid;* (adv) *lower, inferior*

unterbrechen (iv) *to interrupt*

die Unterbrechung (-en) *interruption*

sich unterhalten *to talk, to enjoy oneself*

unterhaltend *entertaining, amusing*

die Unterhose (-n) *drawers, underpants*

unterirdisch *underground*

unternehmen (iv) *to undertake*

das Unternehmen (-) *undertaking*

der **Unterricht** (-e) *instruction, teaching*

unterscheiden (i) *to distinguish, differentiate*

der **Unterschied** (-e) *distinction, difference*

unterschreiben (i) *to sign, put a signature to*

die **Unterschrift** (-en) *signature*

untersuchen *to examine, look into*

die **Untersuching** (-en) *investigation*

die **Untertasse** (-en) *saucer*

die **Unterwäsche** *underclothes*

das **Urteil** (-e) *judgement, sentence, decision*

urteilen *to judge*

V

der **Vater** (-̈) *father*

verachten *to despise*

die **Verachtung** *scorn, contempt, disdain*

verändern *to change, alter*

veranlassen *to cause, to give rise to*

der **Verband** (-̈e) *bandage, union, federation*

verbergen (iv) *to hide, conceal*

verbessern *to improve, amend*

die **Verbesserung** (-en) *improvement, correction*

verbieten (ii) + dat. *to forbid*

verbinden (iii) *to unite, join*

die **Verbindung** (-en) *connection, alliance, student society*

verboten *forbidden*

das **Verbrechen** (-) *crime*

verbreiten (ii) *to spread*

verbrennen (irr. see p. 50) *to burn*

der **Verdacht** *suspicion*

verdächtig *suspicious*

verdächtigen *to suspect*

verdecken *to hide*

verderben (iv) *to spoil*

verdienen *to earn, deserve*

der **Verdienst** (-e) *earnings, profit*

der **Verein** (-e) *union, club, society*

vereinen *to unite, join*

vereinfachen *to simplify*

die **Vereinigten Staaten** *The United States*

der **Verfasser** (-) *author*

verfließen (ii) *to pass (of time)*

verfolgen *to pursue, persecute, prosecute*

die **Vergangenheit** *past*

vergeben (v) (+dat) *to forgive*

vergebens *in vain*

vergessen (v) *to forget*

vergnügen *to enjoy*

das **Vergnügen** (-) *pleasure*

das **Verhältnis** (-se) *relation(ship), affair*

sich **verheiraten** *to get married to*

das **Verhör** (-e) *trial (in court)*

sich **verirren** *to lose one's way, go astray*

verkaufen *to sell*

der **Verkehr** *traffic*

verlangen *to demand, to ask for*

verlassen (vii) *to leave (a place)*

sich **verlassen** (auf) *to rely, depend (on)*

die **Verlegenheit** (-en) *embarrassment, dilemma*

verletzen *to hurt, injure*

verlieren (ii) *to lose*

die **Verlobung** (-en) *engagement, betrothal*

der **Verlust** (-e) *loss*

vermieten *to let, to hire out*

vermissen *to miss, want*

das **Vermögen** (-) *wealth, property, ability*

vermutlich *probable(ly)*

verneinen *to deny*

vernichten *to destroy*

verpassen *to lose (miss) by delay (train, bus)*

sich versammeln *to assemble, gather together*

die Versammlung (-en) *assembly, meeting*

verschaffen *to procure, acquire*

verschieben (ii) *to postpone*

verschieden *different, diverse, various*

die Verschiedenheit (-en) *difference*

verschließen (ii) *to lock up*

verschreiben (i) *to prescribe*

verschwenden *to squander, waste*

verschwinden (iii) *to disappear*

versichern *to insure*

die Versicherung (-en) *insurance*

die Verspätung (-en) *delay*

versprechen (iv) *to promise*

der Verstand *intelligence, understanding*

verständig *intelligent, sensible, wise*

verständlich *understandable, comprehensible*

verstehen *to understand*

verstimmt *out of tune, in a bad humour*

der Versuch (ᵉe) *attempt, trial*

versuchen *to try, attempt*

die Versuchung (-en) *temptation*

verteidigen *to defend*

der Vertrag (-e) *contract, treaty*

vertrauen (+ dat) *to rely on, to trust*

vertreten (v) *to represent*

der Vertreter (-) *representative, agent*

verursachen *to cause, occasion*

die Verwaltung (-en) *administration, management*

der Verwandte (a.n.) *relative, relation*

8—B.E.G.

verwandt *related, allied*

verweigern *to refuse*

verwenden *to apply, use*

verwunden *to wound*

verzeihen (i)(+ dat) *to pardon, excuse*

Verzeihen Sie! *Pardon me*

die Verzeihung (-en) *pardon*

Ich bitte um Verzeihung *I beg your pardon*

verzögern *to delay*

die Verzögerung (-en) *delay*

verzollen *to declare at the Customs*

der Vetter (-n) (w.n.) *cousin*

das Vieh *cattle*

viel *much, many, very, very much*

vielleicht *perhaps*

vielmehr *rather*

das Viertel (-) *quarter, fourth part*

vierteljährlich *quarterly*

die Viertelstunde (-n) *quarter of an hour*

viertens *fourthly*

die Violine (-n) *violin*

das Visum (Visen) *visa*

der Vogel (ᵉ) *bird*

das Volk (ᵉer) *people, nation, race*

die Volksausgabe (-n) *popular edition (of book)*

voll *full, complete*

die Vollendung (-en) *completion*

völlig *fully, completely*

vollkommen *perfect, complete*

von (+ dat) *from, of*

vor-behalten *to reserve*

vorbei *past, over, done, gone*

Es ist vorbei *It's over*

vor-bereiten *to prepare (work, lesson)*

die Vorbereitung (-en) *preparation*

vorgestern *day before yesterday*

der Vorhang (ᵉe) *curtain*

vorher *before (in time)*

vor-kommen *to happen, to occur, to seem, to appear*
Es kommt mir so vor *It seems
to me to be so*
der Vormittag (-e) *morning*
vormittags *in the morning*
vorn (adv) *in the front*
von vorne an *from the beginning*
vornehm *of rank, distinguished*
der Vorrat (⸚e) *provision(s), store,
stock*
der Vorschlag (⸚e) *suggestion, pro-
posal*
die Vorsicht *caution*
Vorsicht! *Look out!*
vor-stellen *to introduce*
sich vor-stellen *to imagine*
die Vorstellung (-en) *performance,
presentation*
der Vorteil (-e) *advantage, profit*
vorüber *by, past, finished*
der Vorwand (⸚e) *pretext, excuse*
vorwärts *forward*

W

die Waage (-n) *balance, scales*
wach *awake, on the alert*
wachen (1) *to wake, be awake;*
(2) *to guard, keep watch over*
das Wachs (-e) *wax*
wachsen (vi) *to grow*
der Wächter (-) *watchman*
die Waffe (-n) *weapon*
der Wagen (-) *car, carriage, coach,
truck*
wagen *to dare, venture*
wägen *to weigh, to balance*
die Wahl (-en) *choice, election*
wählen *to choose, elect*
wahr *true*
Nicht wahr? *Isn't that (it) so?*
währen *to last, endure*
während (+ gen) *during, while*

die Wahrheit (-en) *truth*
wahrscheinlich *probably*
der Wald (⸚er) *forest*
die Wand (⸚e) *(inside) wall*
wandern *to roam, wander, to
hike*
die Wange (-n) *cheek*
wann? *when?* (see p. 55)
Seit wann? *How long ago?*
die Ware (-n) *goods;* pl *merchandise*
warm *warm*
die Wärme *warmth, heat*
warnen *to warn*
die Warnung (-en) *warning*
warten (auf) *to wait (for)*
der Wartesaal *waiting-room (railway)*
das Wartezimmer   *waiting-room
(doctor's, dentist's)*
warum? *why?*
was *what*
was ... auch *whatever ...*
die Wäsche *washing, laundry*
waschen (vi) *to wash*
das Wasser *water*
die Watte (-n) *cotton wool*
wechseln *to change, exchange*
wecken (v tr) *to wake up,
awaken*
der Wecker (-) *alarm clock*
weder ... noch *neither ... nor*
der Weg (-e) *way, path, walk, road*
aus dem Wege gehen *to go
(get) out of one's way*
weg *away*
wegen (+ gen) *on account of*
weh tun *to cause pain, to hurt,
to grieve*
Es tut weh *it hurts*
wehen *to blow (of wind)*
die Wehr *defence*
sich wehren *to defend oneself*
weich *soft, weak*
sich weigern *to object, to refuse*
weil *because* (see p. 54)

die Weihnachten (pl) *Christmas*
der Wein (-e) *wine*
der Weinberg (-e) *vineyard*
weinen *to cry, weep*
die Weise (-n) *way, manner, mode*
  auf keine Weise *in no way*
weisen (i) *to point out, to show*
weiß *white*
weit *far, far off, distant*
  und so weiter *and so on*
welch (-er, -e, -es) *who, which,*
  that (see p. 11)
die Welle (-n) *wave*
die Welt (-en) *world, globe*
die Weltanschauung (-en) *view of*
  life, philosophy of life
die Weltstadt (¨e) *metropolis, city*
wenden (irr. p. 50) *to turn, turn*
  about
wenig *little (of quantity)*
wenige *few*
wenigstens *at least*
wenn *if, when* (see p. 55)
wer *who*
werden (iv) *to become, get, be*
  (see pp. 36, 39, 40)
werfen (iv) *to throw*
das Werk (-e) *work, works (fac-*
  tory)
die Werkstatt (¨en) *workshop*
der Wert (-e) *worth, value*
  wert sein *to be worth*
wertlos *worthless*
wertvoll *valuable*
das Wesen (-) *being, creature*
die Weste (-n) *waistcoat*
der Westen *west*
westlich *western*
wetten *to bet, wager*
das Wetter (-) *weather*
wichtig *important*
die Wichtigkeit (-en) *importance*
wickeln *to wrap*
wider (+ acc) *against, in oppos-*
  ition to

der Widerstand *resistance*
widerstehen *to resist, withstand*
wie *how, as, like*
So ... wie *As ... as ...*
wieder *again, back*
wiederholen *to repeat*
wiederum *again*
wiegen (ii) *to weigh*
die Wiese (-n) *meadow, pasture*
wieviel *how much*
wild *wild, fierce, angry, waste,*
  uncultivated
der Wille (w.n.) *will*
der Wind (-e) *wind, breeze*
winken *to wink, to make a sign,*
  to beckon
der Winter (-) *winter*
wirken *to act, have an effect*
die Wirkung (-en) *effect*
der Wirt (-e) *landlord, host*
die Wirtin (-nen) *landlady, hostess*
die Wirtschaft (-en) *economy,*
  housekeeping
das Wirtshaus (¨er) *inn, tavern, pub*
wischen *to wipe*
wissen (wußte, gewußt, ich weiß,
  er weiß) *to know (by learn-*
  ing, experience
das Wissen *knowledge*
die Wissenschaft (-en) *science*
die Witwe (-n) *widow*
der Witwer *widower*
der Witz (-e) *joke*
wo *where*
wobei *by which*
die Woche (-n) *week*
wöchentlich *weekly*
wodurch *through which, where-*
  by
wofür *why, what, for what*
Wofür halten Sie mich? *What*
  do you take me for?
wogegen *against which, what*
woher *where from*
wohin *where to*

wohl *well*
wohnen *to dwell*
die Wohnung (-en) *dwelling, flat*
das Wohnzimmer *living-room*
die Wolke (-n) *cloud*
die Wolle (-n) *wool*
wollen *to wish, to want* (see pp. 41-2)
womit *wherewith, with which*
wonach *after which*
woran *at which, whereat*
worauf *on which, whereupon*
woraus *out of, from which*
worin *wherein, in which*
das Wort *word*
(pl) die Wörter *words* (separately) die Worte *words* (collectively)
das Wörterbuch (⸚er) *dictionary*
das Wörterverzeichnis *list of words*
wörtlich *word for word, literally*
der Wortschatz *vocabulary*
worüber *over (above) which*
worum *about what*
worunter *under which*
wovon *of what, which*
wozu *for what, why, to, for which*
die Wunde (-n) *wound*
das Wunder (-) *wonder, miracle*
wunderbar *wonderful(ly)*
sich wundern *to be surprised*
wunderschön *beautiful(ly), wonderful(ly)*
der Wunsch (⸚e) *wish, desire*
wünschen *to wish, desire, to want*
würdig *worthy, dignified*
die Wurst (⸚e) *sausage*
die Wurzel (-n) *root*
die Wut *rage, anger*
wüten *to be in a rage, to rage*
wütend *angry, furious*

Z

zähe *tough (of meat), tenacious, grasping*
die Zahl (-en) *number*
zahlen *to pay*
zählen *to count*
die Zahlung (-en) *payment*
der Zahn (⸚e) *tooth*
der Zahnarzt (⸚e) *dentist*
die Zahnbürste (-n) *toothbrush*
die Zahnpasta *tooth paste*
das Zahnweh *toothache*
der Zank *quarrel*
sich zanken *to quarrel, wrangle*
zart *soft, delicate*
der Zauber (-) *magic, enchantment, charm*
die Zehe (-n) *toe*
das Zeichen (-) *sign, mark, token, symptom*
zeichnen *to draw, sketch*
zeigen *to show*
der Zeiger (-) *hand (of clock)*
die Zeile (-en) *(printed) line*
die Zeit (-en) *time*
zur Zeit *at present*
zeitig *early*
die Zeitkarte (-n) *season ticket*
die Zeitschrift (-en) *periodical, magazine*
die Zeitung (-en) *newspaper*
die Zelle (-n) *cell, booth, kiosk*
das Zelt (-e) *tent*
der/das Zentimeter *0·394 ins.*
zentral *central*
zer- (prefix indicates) *asunder* (with violence)
zerbrechen (iv) *to smash (glass etc.), to burst*
zerreißen (i) *to tear up, tear to pieces*
zerschlagen (vi) *to beat, break to pieces*
zerschneiden (i) *to cut to pieces*

zerstören *to destroy*
der **Zettel** (-) *scrap of paper, label, note*
ziehen (ii) *to pull draw, haul*
das **Ziel** (-e) *target, aim, end, limit*
ziemlich (adv) *rather, somewhat*
ziemlich oft *pretty often*
die **Ziffer** (-n) *figure, cipher*
die **Zigarre** (-n) *cigar*
die **Zigarette** (-n) *cigarette*
das **Zimmer** (-) *room*
der **Zimmermann** (pl -leute) *carpenter*
zittern *to tremble, vibrate*
der **Zoll** (¨e) *toll, tax, customs duty*
das **Zollamt** (¨er) *customs office*
der **Zollbeamte** (a.n.) *customs officer*
zollfrei *duty-free*
die **Zone** (-n) *zone*
zornig *angry, furious*
zu (prep + dat) *to, at, in, on,* (adv) *too*
zu Hause *at home*
der **Zucker** *sugar*
zu-decken *to cover*
zuerst *at first*
zufällig *by chance*
zufrieden *content, pleased, satisfied*
der **Zug** (¨e) *train, draught*
zugänglich *open, accessible*

zu-geben *to admit, confess*
zugleich *at the same time*
zu-hören (+ dat) *to listen to*
die **Zukunft** *future*
zu-lassen *to allow*
zuletzt *at last*
zu-machen *to shut, close*
zunächst *at first*
die **Zunge** (-n) *tongue*
zurecht *ready, in good order*
zurück (adv) *back, backwards,* (sep prefix)
zurück-kehren *to turn back, return*
zusammen (adv and sep prefix) *together, altogether*
die **Zusammenkunft** *meeting, encounter, convention*
der **Zuschauer** (-) *spectator,* (pl) *audience*
zwar *certainly, indeed, it's true*
der **Zweck** (-e) *purpose*
zweierlei *of two kinds, different*
zweifach *twofold*
der **Zweifel** (-) *doubt*
zweifeln *to doubt*
der **Zweig** (-e) *twig, branch*
zweitens *secondly*
zwingen (iii) *to force, compel*
zwischen (+ dat/acc) *between, among*
der **Zwist** (über) *dissension, discord, dispute* (*over, about*)

Common German abbreviations

Abt.	Abteilung	department; section
AG.	Aktiengesellschaft	joint stock company
Bez.	Bezirk	district
d.J.	dieses Jahres	this year
d.M.	dieses Monats	this month
DM.	Deutsche Mark	German Mark
Ges.	Gesellschaft	company

G.m.b.H.	Gesellschaft mit beschränkter Haftung	limited liability company
Hbf.	Hauptbahnhof	main station (railway)
i.allg.	im allgemeinen	in general
I.G.	Interessengemeinschaft	trust; cartel
Kap.	Kapitel	chapter
M.E.Z.	mitteleuropäische Zeit	Central European Time
usw.	und so weiter	and so on; et cetera

Metric weights and measures

Lineal measure

das Meter   meter
1 Zentimeter (cm)=0·39 inch
10 cm=about 4 inches
30 cm=1 foot
1 Meter=39·37 inches   11 Meter=12 yards
1 Kilometer=0·621 mile
 8 Km=about 5 miles
20 Km=12½ miles
50 Km=31 miles

Square measure

der or **das Ar, -es, pl Are**
1 Ar=100 sq. meters (40½ Are=1 acre)
1 Quadratmeter (=3·95 poles).
1 Hektar (10,000 sq. meters)=about 2½ acres

Weights

das Gramm (g.) **-s, pl Gramme**
28⅓ gramm=1 ounce
1 Hektogramm=about 3½ ounces
1 Kilogramm=2·204 lb.
5 Kilogramm=11 lb.

Fluid Measure

das Liter pl Liter—1·76 pints
4½ Liter—1 gallon
1 Dekaliter=slightly over 2 gallons
1 Hektoliter—about 22 gallons

PART III

EXTRACTS TO ILLUSTRATE THE USE AND SCOPE OF THE VOCABULARY AND GRAMMAR

PART TWO

EXTRACTS TO ILLUSTRATE THE USE AND SCOPE OF THE VOCABULARY AND GRAMMAR

1. A tale from the Folklore Collection of the Brothers Grimm[1]

Der Wolf und der Mensch
The Wolf and the Man

Der Fuchs erzählte einmal dem Wolf von der
The fox once told the wolf about the

Stärke des Menschen. Kein Tier könnte ihm
strength of man. No animal could

widerstehen, und sie müßten List gebrauchen,
stand up against him, and they must use cunning

um sich vor ihm zu erhalten. Da antwortete,
to protect themselves from him. Then answered

der Wolf: 'Wenn ich nur einmal einen
the wolf: 'If I could only once get to see a

Menschen zu sehen bekäme, würde ich doch auf
man, I would fly at him

ihn losgehen.' 'Dazu kann ich dir helfen.'
nevertheless.' 'In that I can help you.'

sprach der Fuchs, 'komm nur morgen früh
said the fox, 'Just come to me to-morrow morning,

zu mir, so will ich dir einen zeigen.' Der
and I will show you one.'   The

Wolf stellte sich frühzeitig ein, und der Fuchs
wolf presented himself early,   and the fox

brachte ihn hinaus auf den Weg, den der Jäger
brought him out on the road which the hunter

---

[1] The extract from Grimm, and that on page 114 (taken with permission from *The Observer* of 5th February 1933), demonstrate the flexibility and scope of the instrument provided. Both can be tackled with hardly any need for reference to a dictionary. The next extract from Einstein's *Relativity* is, of course, more difficult: but, it will soon be realized, the difficulties are more in the *ideas* than in the *words*. The intelligent adult student should be able to deal quite well with it, if he knows his 'Basis and Essentials'.

alle Tage ging. Zuerst kam ein alter abgedankter
daily walked. First came an old discharged

Soldat. 'Ist das ein Mensch?' fragte der
soldier. 'Is that a man?' asked the

Wolf. 'Nein,' antwortete der Fuchs, 'das
wolf. 'No,' answered the fox, 'that was

ist einer gewesen.' Danach kam ein kleiner
one once.' After that came a small

Knabe, der zur Schule wollte. 'Ist das ein
boy on the way to school. 'Is that a

Mensch?' 'Nein, das will erst einer werden.'
man?' 'No, that will become one soon.'

Endlich kam der Jäger, die Doppelflinte auf dem
At last came the hunter, with double-barrelled gun on his

Rücken und den Hirschfänger an der Seite.
back and hunting-knife at his side.

Sprach der Fuchs zum Wolf: 'Siehst du,
Said the fox to the wolf: 'Look,

dort kommt ein Mensch; auf den mußt du
there comes a man; it's him you have to

losgehen, ich aber will mich fort in meine
go for, but I will make off to my

Höhle machen.' Der Wolf ging nun auf den
lair.'   The wolf now went for the

Menschen los. Der Jäger, als er ihn erblickte,
man.   The hunter, when he saw him,

sprach: 'Es ist schade, daß ich keine Kugel
said: 'It is a pity that I have not loaded

geladen habe,' legte an und schoß dem Wolf
with bullets,' took aim and fired the small-shot at the wolf's

das Schrot ins Gesicht. Der Wolf verzog das
face.   The wolf twisted his

Gesicht gewaltig, doch ließ er sich nicht
face violently, though he did not let himself

schrecken und ging vorwärts; da gab ihm der
be frightened and went ahead: then the

Jäger die zweite Ladung. Der Wolf verbiß
hunter gave him the second charge. The wolf suppressed

den Schmerz und rückte dem Jäger zu Leibe;
the pain and closed up on the hunter;

da zog dieser seinen blanken Hirschfänger und
whereupon the latter drew his bright hunting-knife and

gab ihm links und rechts ein paar Hiebe, daß
gave him left and right a few cuts, so that,

er, über und über blutend, mit Geheul zu dem
bleeding all over, he ran howling back to

Fuchs zurücklief. 'Nun, Bruder Wolf,' sprach
the fox.   'Now, brother wolf,' said

der Fuchs, 'wie bist du mit dem Menschen
the fox, 'how did you deal with the man?'

fertig geworden?' 'Ach,' antwortete der
'Oh,' answered the

Wolf, 'so hab' ich mir die Stärke des Menschen
wolf, 'I hadn't imagined the strength of man

nicht vorgestellt, erst nahm er einen Stock
to be such: first he took a stick

von der Schulter und blies hinein, da flog mir
from his shoulder and blew into it, whereupon

etwas ins Gesicht; das hat mich ganz entsetzlich gekitzelt.
something flew into my face; that tickled me horribly.

Danach pustete er noch einmal in den Stock,
After that he blew once again into the stick,

da zog mir's um die Nase, wie Blitz
and something flew round my nose like lightning

und Hagelwetter, und wie ich ganz nah war,
and hail, and as I was quite near,

da zog er eine blanke Rippe aus dem Leib;
he drew a bright rib from his body;

damit hat er so auf mich losgeschlagen, daß
with this he so attacked me that

ich beinah tot wäre liegen geblieben.' 'Siehst
I almost got killed (remained lying dead).' ' You see,'

du,' sprach der Fuchs, 'was du für ein Prahlhans
said the fox, 'what (sort of) a braggart you

bist, du wirfst das Beil so weit, daß du's
are, you fling the hatchet so far that you

nicht wieder holen kannst.'
can't fetch it back.'

2. An extract from *The Observer*

The Craft of the Nailsmith

Das Handwerk des Nagelschmiedes

In spite of all mechanical inventions there still remains in the South of Germany a place for the nailsmith.

It is true that this industry is dying out, and only recently the news was received of the cessation after fifty years' practice of his handicraft of the last wholetime 'nailer' in Bavaria.

There continues, however, to be a small demand, which has unexpectedly increased in recent years, for hand-worked nails for mountaineering boots, and in one or two Bavarian mountain hamlets, and also in parts of the Thuringian and Bohemian forests, this industry is still carried on as a seasonal job in the winter by men who in the

Trotz aller mechanischen Erfindungen bleibt im Süden Deutschlands noch Platz für den Nagelschmied.

Zwar stirbt das Gewerbe aus, und erst kürzlich erhielt man die Nachricht, daß der letzte vollberufliche 'Nagler' in Bayern nach fünfzigjähriger Ausübung sein Handwerk aufgegeben hat.

Es gibt aber noch immer eine geringe Nachfrage nach handgearbeiteten Nägeln für Bergstiefel, die in den letzten Jahren unerwarteterweise zugenommen hat; und in einigen bayrischen Bergdörfern, sowie in Teilen des Thüringer and des Böhmer Waldes wird dieses Gewerbe noch im Winter von Männern ausgeübt, die in den

summer months work as carpenters, shepherds, wood-carvers, and mountain guides.	Sommermonaten als Tischler, Hirten, Holzschnitzer und Bergführer arbeiten.

summer months work as
carpenters, shepherds, wood-
carvers, and mountain guides.

In the smithies, some of which
are very old, the methods of
work have not altered since the
forges were set up one hundred
and fifty years ago.

A nailsmith working, as he
usually does, for some twelve to
thirteen hours daily, incidentally
for very low wages, can turn out
between 1000 and 1100 nails of
the smaller variety.

The nails, which are retailed
through the sports shops in the
towns, apparently find their
greatest foreign outlet in Austria
and Switzerland.

Sommermonaten als Tischler,
Hirten, Holzschnitzer und
Bergführer arbeiten.

In den Schmieden, von denen
manche sehr alt sind, haben sich
die Arbeitsmethoden nicht
geändert, seit die Essen vor
hundertfünfzig Jahren gesetzt
wurden.

Ein Nagelschmied, der wie
üblich etwa zwölf bis dreizehn
Stunden täglich arbeitet—
übrigens für sehr niedrigen
Lohn—kann tausend bis
elfhundert Nägel der kleineren
Sorten herstellen.

Die Nägel, die durch die
Sportgeschäfte in den Städten
verkauft werden, finden
anscheinend den größten
ausländischen Absatz in
Österreich und der Schweiz.

3. Extract from the works of Einstein[1]

Spezielles und allgemeines Relativitätsprinzip.

Special and General Theory of Relativity

Nachdem sich die Einführung des speziellen Relativitätsprinzips bewährt hat, muß es jedem nach Verallgemeinerung strebenden Geiste verlockend erscheinen, den Schritt zum allgemeinen Relativitätsprinzip zu wagen.

Since the introduction of the special principle of relativity has proved itself, every intellect which strives after generalization must feel the temptation to venture the step towards the general principle of relativity.

[1] With acknowledgment to the author and his publishers (*Über die spezielle und allgemeine Relativitätstheorie:* Von Albert Einstein. Sammlung Vieweg). English edition: *RELATIVITY: The Special and General Theory.* By Albert Einstein. Authorized translation (from which the above version is taken) by Dr. R. W. Lawson, published by Methuen and Co. Ltd., 1920).

Aber eine einfache, scheinbar ganz zuverlässige Betrachtung läßt einen solchen Versuch zunächst aussichtslos erscheinen.

Der Leser denke sich in den schon so oft betrachteten, gleichförmig fahrenden Eisenbahnwagen versetzt. Solange der Wagen gleichförmig fährt, ist für den Insassen nichts vom Fahren des Wagens zu merken. Daher kommt es auch, daß der Insasse den Tatbestand ohne inneres Widerstreben dahin deuten kann, daß der Wagen ruhe, der Bahndamm aber bewegt sei. Diese Interpretation ist übrigens nach dem speziellen Relativitätsprinzip auch physikalisch ganz berechtigt.

Wird nun aber die Bewegung des Wagens etwa dadurch in eine ungleichförmige verwandelt, daß der Wagen kräftig gebremst wird, so erhält der Insasse einen entsprechend kräftigen Ruck nach vorne. Die beschleunigte Bewegung des Wagens äußert sich in dem mechanischen Verhalten der Körper relativ zu ihm; das mechanische Verhalten ist ein andres als im vorhin betrachteten Falle, und es erscheint deshalb ausgeschlossen zu sein, daß relativ zum *ungleichförmig* bewegten Wagen die gleichen mechanischen Gesetze gelten, wie relativ zum

But a simple and apparently quite reliable consideration seems to suggest that, for the present at any rate, there is little hope of success in such an attempt.

Let us imagine ourselves transferred to our old friend the railway carriage, which is travelling at a uniform rate. As long as it is moving uniformly, the occupant of the carriage is not sensible of its motion, and it is for this reason that he can unreluctantly interpret the facts of the case as indicating that the carriage is at rest, but the embankment in motion. Moreover, according to the special principle of relativity, this interpretation is quite justified also from a physical point of view.

If the motion of the carriage is now changed into a non-uniform motion, as for instance by a powerful application of the brakes, then the occupant of the carriage experiences a correspondingly powerful jerk forwards. The retarded motion is manifested in the mechanical behaviour of bodies relative to the person in the railway carriage. The mechanical behaviour is different from that of the case previously considered, and for this reason it would appear to be impossible that the same mechanical laws hold relatively to the non-uniformly moving carriage, as hold with reference

ruhenden beziehungsweise gleichförmig bewegten Wagen.

Jedenfalls ist klar, daß relativ zum ungleichförmig bewegten Wagen der Galileische Grundsatz nicht gilt. Wir fühlen uns daher zunächst genötigt, entgegen dem allgemeinen Relativitätsprinzip der ungleichförmigen Bewegung eine Art absolute physikalische Realität zuzusprechen. Im folgenden werden wir aber bald sehen, daß dieser Schluß nicht stichhaltig ist.

to the carriage when at rest or in uniform motion.

At all events it is clear that the Galileian law does not hold with respect to the non-uniformly moving carriage. Because of this, we feel compelled at the present juncture to grant a kind of absolute physical reality to non-uniform motion, in opposition to the general principle of relativity. But in what follows we shall soon see that this conclusion cannot be maintained.

The word **Beschleunigung** in physics (as here) is applied to change of velocity, whether acceleration or retardation.